NEVER STOP WINNING Vol. 1
Win Your Way

Willie J.

Copyright © 2024 WILLIE J. All rights reserved. No part of this book can be reproduced in any form without the written permission of the author and its publisher.

Table of Contents

Introduction:	13
Dreaming Big In a Toxic Environment	25
My Winners Mindset	43
The Origin of Creation	57
I'm Growing To Win	71
Winning Habits	89
My Drive to Win (Driven)	127
Failing To Win	143
Faith Over Fear	155
Forgiveness Is Freedom, Bitterness Is Bondage	175
Growing Under Pressure	189
My Entrepreneurial Advice in Forbes and GQ	205
Resilience Is Brilliance	211
A Call to Action:	233
Dedications & Thank You's:	235

A QUICK NOTE TO MYSELF:

Everyone in this life needs to be reminded from time to time. So, I tend to remind myself every day.

Good morning, good morning, Willie J.

Rise and shine my dear brother.

So how are we feeling today sir? Did you get some good ole sleep last night? Or did you have some good ole dreams about your future plans for tomorrow?

Well, I hope that you did.

Because I believe that today is going to be a very good day for you my friend, I just know that it will.

I can actually feel it deeply within my soul. My mental climate is starting to shift gears with an intense aura elevating me far beyond its usual control. Wow!

Can you feel it in the air? Wow! Can you really feel it in the air? I know that I can.

Which sort of reminds me of a hit record made by the legendary Phil Collins entitled "Feel it in the air tonight."
Now the fresh winds are blowing intensely, and the trees are clapping loudly and proudly with a multitude of celebrations.

As they cheer you on so faithfully to chant you abroad, saying, "Go Willie J. you can do this bro, come on Willie J. you can do this bro, and even better than you did yesterday."

For it is a new day and a new way. So just keep on climbing up that ladder of success bro, but wait, first we must pray.

At last, we finally meet up again, with yet another golden opportunity at hand. To breathe in some of your fresh winds. Then to level up with a brand-new chance to win big.

Well, I heard that fear and failure came by your house late last night. To rest up in preparation for tomorrow's early flight.

However, the truth of the matter is that they were both worried about you, and we're just hoping and praying that you are doing well and alright. They said that they had only come along to help you grow rich, wealthy, and strong like a thief drifting away through the night. To help you succeed beyond your wildest dreams, and to hopefully remind you that the things on this earth aren't always the way that they seem.

So, please stay focused Willie J. and continue to win big from the inside out!

Introduction:

We are currently living in a dark cold world, where there is so much hate, so much fear, so much turmoil, so much division and so much uncertainty. Meanwhile, the need for more love, more unity, more hope, and more peace is at an all-time high.

With brutal wars unfolding right before our very eyes. We are desperately crying out loud for our greatest leaders and our bravest warriors to finally arise. To finally take their rightful places, stages, and positions in a time where the mindsets of everyone are under immense attacks.

It is no secret that we are all being forced into a certain way of thinking whether we agree with it or not. They program us to deny our own opinions in fear of being canceled, and even worse becoming mentally enslaved, and I like to call this mental slavery.

However, we all have the human tendency to want acceptance at times, but the danger

is that we find ourselves just going along to get along while singing the same ole repetitive songs. Which is extremely frustrating to me. Why?
For the simple fact that I was never created to be a premium member of this *Get Along Gang Chorale* to begin with. Lol

Can you feel me? Have you ever felt this way before? Well, I'm sure that you have.

See, society rarely teaches us that being our true authentic selves is always good enough. When in fact it is the only way to be. We were all uniquely handcrafted by God, and were created to be unique, and stick out amongst the big crowds.

Unfortunately, most of us in today's culture have become the modern-day filters of society, and we wear disguises in hopes of hiding who we truly are inside. We often compare ourselves to one another, only to forget that comparison is the real thief of joy and peace.

Now why is that you may ask?

Well, I believe that it is mainly due to this new phenomenon that we call social media. Which is basically the modern media of today's world. A dark web where most individuals are beyond afraid of being themselves while pretending to be someone that they're not.

The naked truth of the matter is that we are all imperfect human beings, and human beings are simply beings that were created to be human.

Now with that being said, I can recall feeling the exact same way inside. Fearing failure and fearing loss at all human cost.

In a blurry moment when I couldn't comprehend that all big winners in life had to fail at first. Which sort of reminds me of a great quote made by the legendary Michael Jordan who said that:

"To learn to succeed you must first learn to fail." In other words, allow your failures to teach you how to win. That's right!

Learn how to fail now in order to win later, and I can clearly see that my biggest failures in life were actually paving the way for me to win bigger, and to keep on winning forward. Yes sir!

Even in the midst of one of the deadliest pandemics ever known to mankind. We would still find a way to win big and defeat this horrible virus called Covid-19, and I just thank God for the grace.

A very brutal and vicious virus that would kill millions of people from around the globe, including a few close friends of mine. In a time when most small businesses and startup companies collapsed and died. This ironically became the beginning of me and my company's greatest victories.

The world-renowned Pure Mission Entertainment (PME) was officially born, and we were really starting to turn all our greatest pains into our greatest gains. This is why I often use the terminology of hope.

"Pain is Gain"

In the beginning me and my business partner Aaron Emig would meet up regularly in our hometowns to go over some winning game plans and new strategies.

We would consistently come together every week to mastermind over some creative concepts and innovative ideas in the grass roots.

Unfortunately, before having our first meeting. I suddenly got into a near fatal car accident which nearly killed me, and I watched my whole life flash right before my blurry eyes.
"Boy, oh boy I was so beyond crushed and bruised, and I was also very terrified for my life."

I can clearly recall seeing the picture of a bright beaming light flashing right across my dashboard, and I must admit that I was in deep shock.

Because I really couldn't believe that this could happen to someone in the name of trying to do a good deed, and I felt like I was being punished somehow for trying to do so. It just didn't make any ethical sense to me at the time, and to be totally honest I became a little bitter inside.

Why?

Well, for starters I was prescribed to take four or more painkillers throughout every waking moment of the day. Just to get through it, and man let me tell you, it was a very bad situation for your boy.

However, at the same time I was just grateful to God for miraculously sparing my life, and for allowing me another chance to fulfill the rest of my destiny and dreams.

Now, we just finished recording and releasing my company's first hit single entitled "We Love You Puerto Rico" featuring Various Artists. A smash hit record that eventually went #2 on the Top

200 European International Indie music charts.

It was a very passionate record that I was asked to write, produce and perform in dedication to all the Hurricane Maria victims. Which ended up gaining millions of streams worldwide, along with a ton of global donations near and far. It was a huge success to say the least.

This charity-based record was produced by me and my bros Louis, and Theo Harden, who goes by the name of Muzic Doctors. It was performed by me, my beautiful daughter Jazmine Jones, Crystal Haywood, Jade, Latonya Johnson, and 4x Olympic world boxing champ and client, Arthur Flash Johnson.

Shortly afterwards, I was asked to write another charity-based hit record entitled "In the Morning." A very heartfelt Journey sampled anthem dedicated to all the wounded victims of Covid-19. Which gained over 10 million streams and over 1 million TikTok streams globally.

This massive hit single featured one of my best friends and artist Terry Sanford on the background vocals, who unfortunately passed away before it could ever be released. RIP bro.

Since then, my music has accumulated 28 million plus streams globally in over 184 countries, and I have been seen on major platforms like Broadway World, ABC30, CBS, FOX, NBC, Forbes Magazine, GQ Magazine, and YAHOO! Business Insider, The Source, XXL, NY Times Square Billboard, MTV and many more.

Along with a prestigious honor to be featured in the #1 spot of the LA Weekly's Top 10 Amazing Innovators Revolutionizing Their Industry. They also featured me as a Top Entrepreneur to Watch in 2023.

Immediately after that I received another coveted #1 spot in the LA Wire Top 10 Entrepreneurs of 2023, which featured the financial legends Warren Buffet, Bill Gates,

Michael Bloomberg, Mark Zuckerberg and many more.

Which led to me being featured on the front covers of four global magazines all within the same year. The Los Angeles Business Magazine, Stardom Magazine, Celebrity Forbes Magazine, and The Morocco Forbes Magazine. Who also featured a review of my hit single "Never Let U GO." A very sentimental record that I dedicated to all the earthquake victims of Morocco. RIP

We were really on the move now with an amazing interview feature with the incredible Dr. Forbes Riley on her amazing award winning "Forbes Factor" Radio Podcast, along with being featured on the digital cover in the #1 spot of the NY Weekly Magazines Top 10 Entrepreneurs of 2024.

Shortly after my follow up feature on the digital cover of the Celebrity Forbes Magazine Top 10 Public Figures to watch for in 2024, and a prestigious feature in the NY Weekly's Magazine Top 10 Emerging Celebrities of 2024: Shaping the Future of

Stardom. With a host of superstars like Beyoncé, Zendaya, Cristiano Ronaldo and more.

I have been blessed to grace stages and be featured in major write ups with famous acts such as Maya Angelou, Kobe Bryant, Mark Twain, TLC, Brian Tracy, CeCe Winans, Justin Bieber, Elon Musk, Rod Wave, Kevin Hart, Martin Lawrence, Kirk Franklin, Will Smith, Floyd Mayweather, Drake, Nicki Minaj, Eminem, and many more.

While most recently I have been the co-author, and featured author of 7 #1 Global Best Selling books. Rattled Awake "Volume One and Two", "A Note to My Family: I Am Your Legacy", "Beyond Boundaries: Thriving in Life's Grey Zone", "Rebel with a Cause", The Book of Human Empowerment "Purpose & Mindset". Along with the global classic anthology "Winning With Love."

The follow up to three of my limited-edition books of poetry which was also nominated into the Who's Who in American Literature several years ago.

I have been the keynote speaker, singer, facilitator, recording artist and musician at international workshops, seminars, and events for leaders and aspiring leaders in places like Taiwan, Pakistan, Europe, and the Philippines.

Now, as an ambassador of the Gospel Music Hall of Fame, a certified speaker, teacher, facilitator, and life coach of the Maxwell leadership team. My goal is to expand my overall reach by empowering and inspiring more people to become their best versions, while awakening the potential within the souls of millions.

See, I don't share any of these miraculous accomplishments with you to sound boastful or braggadocious in any kind of way. However, my true motives are simply to paint a clear vivid picture of hope, and to show you that anything and everything is possible if you can only believe that it is.

That's right, anything is possible with God and hard work.

So, I look forward to sharing some of my most powerful secrets, concepts, ideas, and proven strategies with you. Some of the very tools and commentary that I live by each and every day of my life.

The same winning principles that will allow you to soar right where you are, and to keep you soaring for the rest of your days. As I truly believe that the Creator created us all to win big, and to finally win big beyond our fondest imaginations.

Now let's go winners!

Chapter 1

Dreaming Big In a Toxic Environment

WINNING IN A TOXIC ENVIRONMENT: Everything starts with a God-given vision and dream, and like anyone else, I would have the tendency to allow the toxic nuances of my environment to get the best of me. Until one day I realized that my dreams were much bigger than my environment.

However, my high hopes for living out my biggest dreams became very difficult for me growing up on the brutal streets of East Saint Louis and Washington Park, Illinois.

Because I had been dwelling in a domain where most people settled to live lackluster lifestyles regardless of all the talent and potential they possessed.

We were all deeply rooted in an atmosphere of envy, hate, great depression, oppression, and oftentimes recession, but at times we would still have some of our greatest moments.

Where hood dreams became hood nightmares very quickly. Which was mainly due to a lack of pure purpose, self-love, unity and spiritual vision growing forward, and it is written that,
"Without a vision the people will perish."

So, this had to be one of the core reasons behind us killing one another at such an alarming rate.

Or the main reason why we remain trapped inside of our own matrix, and why we seem to always pull each other down like crabs hanging in a bucket at every chance that we get. Instead of celebrating one another's successes, blessings, and progress.

Well, speaking of some hood nightmares. I can recall witnessing a young man getting killed in the broad daylight in his own backyard, and I'm talking about a real live horror scene here.

Then later I can recall losing a good friend and classmate to more senseless gun violence, who was only 13 years old at the time while attending middle school.

We would often skip classes together, but on that dark fateful day I decided not to, he would be brutally murdered in cold blood.

Talking about being totally blown away with fear, disbelief, and sadness.

However, back in those days I would often sneak away from my friends and family to go write music and poetry, and to privately dream big about being in a real movie someday.

Meanwhile, me and my cousin Me Me would sometimes use my Aunties video camera, to imagine ourselves performing in our own music video on TV.

I mean, you just couldn't pay us to believe that this wasn't going to happen for us one day. It was all just a matter of time, and we even wrote our own movie scripts and books too.

This would essentially become a great mental escape for me as well as a therapeutic means for coping with all the inner city struggles at the time. Simply put, life wasn't always that easy for me growing up, and I am well convinced today that it wasn't supposed to be. So, it's all good.

I had to eventually learn that any big dream worth having in this life would have to be paid forward at a big price.

With a very healthy price that I was willing to pay and sacrifice with my very own life. Along with possessing some good work ethics of course.
Which reminds me of a great quote made by the legendary John C. Maxwell who said that,

"Everything Worth-While is Uphill."

In other words, most people want to live the big dream, but very few people are willing to pay the big price for it. Yep!

Then I can clearly remember one day when my beautiful mom came to me and broke some horrible news about my cousin Tony passing away due to more senseless gun violence. Smh

She was very reluctant to tell me at first. About how he was suddenly gunned down at the age of 21. Meanwhile, I was only 16 years old at the time, and was in deep pursuit of my musical journey, and career.

Man, I was so crushed, and this undoubtedly became a huge spiritual awakening for your boy. Because I just knew deep down inside that I could become the next victim or statistic on that list.

However, Tony would often ask me to come over to his house and bring over my entire musical collection.

Which featured some of the greatest artists of all time, and he encouraged me to dream aloud and to imagine myself performing on that big stage right next to them.

So, it should be no surprise that his death would greatly impact my life in a major way, and that I would never be the same growing forward.

I had to realize that my cousin Tony was put here on this earth. To be one of the ones who would help me to recognize my true talents and potential.

He was sent here to help me understand that I was not a hopeless victim of my environment, and that I could do, be, and have anything I ever wanted out of life. RIP Cuz

MAMA TAUGHT ME HOW TO DREAM BIG: She was always a big dreamer at heart and by nature, and her winner's mindset was very contagious to say the least.

Fortunately, enough, I was blessed with the greatest Mama of all times, the G.O.A.T of all Moms, and that's none other than the legendary (Barbara Ann Jones).

She was a very beautiful multi- talented woman of God who had always loved me unconditionally, and she gradually became one of my greatest mentors.

More importantly, she became my best friend until the end of time. A highly gifted musician who was always there to help me succeed in both worlds. Meaning the spiritual world and the musical world.

When I felt fatigued and almost on the verge of giving up, she gave me new hope, and she always helped me to believe in myself.

She helped me to believe that I could fly high and achieve anything that I had set my mind to, regardless of my environment.

On this one particular day my mom came into my bedroom with some of my greatest high school accomplishments, and she started to place them right above me and upon the walls.

Which was very timely because I had been going through some deep internal struggles. I truly believe with all my heart that this mental maneuver was meant to consciously remind me of who I was, and to show me that my childhood dreams were actually starting to come to pass right before our eyes.
She was showing me how to paint the subconscious mind, and indirectly teaching me how to keep on winning no matter what. Thank you so much mama for allowing God to use you. Rest in Heaven

WHEN MY DREAMS BECAME A NIGHTMARE: So, I woke up one bright morning to tell my mom about a wild dream that I had the previous night. Which was more like a wild nightmare about me being locked up behind bars. A very crazy vision of me getting out on bail as we hugged one another with tears.

She really couldn't believe any of this at first, and I can tell that she found it very hard to decipher and digest. However, she urged me to just relax, stay calm, be cool, and to go and pray about the matter more fervently, but unfortunately two years later this same nightmare manifested and came to pass like a whirlwind out of another cosmos.
Woe!

I ended up facing 6 to 30 years in the maximum penitentiary, and nearly missing out on that golden opportunity of seeing my beautiful daughter Jazmine born. I mean, just like that all my biggest dreams were crushed overnight, and I was starting to feel hopeless about myself to say the least.

My big dreams had suddenly become a nightmare, but then I remembered hearing my beautiful mom's voice ask me so sincerely.

"Is it over now son? Is it over?" And I gently replied to her with courage and tears streaming down my face.

"Yes it is Mama, I'm so done with this lifestyle, it is all over now, and I ain't ever coming back to this dungeon again." As we began to embrace one another tightly.

I am just so grateful today to say that I haven't looked back since then, and that I have been on a new journey of spiritual growth, evolution, and unprecedented success growing forward.

Now, I just had to find a way to repay God and my beautiful Mama for investing so much love into me. Then to show myself that all the painful sacrifices over the years were not made in vain.

To finally reap all the fruits and benefits of all our hard labor, and I'm just so elated that I got to pay it forward. Because my Mom got to see me blossom like a new rose born from under the concrete.

She got to witness me packing out concerts, services, clinics and other major events at venues like the Guitar Center, the Civic Center, and more.

So, I realize now that she had been prepping me all along for success, and it is the sole reason why I often say today that my Mama taught me how to dream big.

TELLING MYSELF STORIES: I soon discovered that I am the narrator of my own big dreams, and not the environment of people surrounding me. I must tell my own story.

While looking back, I can picture my mom tucking me in at night to read me some of my favorite bedtime stories.

Which was a mental technique used by most parents to help their child sleep better, and to ultimately have good dreams.

However, I learned later that these same bedtime stories were actually being stored into the subconscious mind. Inside of that

dark secluded space where all my dreams, fears, and nightmares had lived all along.
It is the land where our belief systems become reality, and it is stated that the subconscious mind can create 95% or more of our results in life. Including our results from buying in the marketplace. Because we typically buy off of impulse.

The Harvard Business school professor Gerald Zaltman says that 95% of our purchase decision making takes place in the subconscious mind.

In other words, whatever stories that are being sold to the subconscious mind whether it be real or fake. Can and will be purchased in our reality. Because this is the place where we make most of our choices and decisions.

I finally came to the realization that this had a lot to do with me making poor decisions, and it was the core reason why I had become a prisoner to my own negative way of thinking. A modern-day slave to my very own thoughts.

Simply because I had been selling myself the wrong stories. Which resulted in me keeping the wrong company at times. It sort of reminds me of a popular quote that says, "We are the company that we keep."
That's right!

We become the company that we keep. So please be very beware of those toxic dream killers who may be surrounding you right now. Because wise men hang with wise men, but a companion of fools will subsequently be destroyed by other fools.

So, I soon discovered that children are the biggest dreamers by nature, and that they always tend to dream big without limits, and on some occasions, they will even have imaginary friends for role play.

We often call this "The Power of the Imagination."

They create their own narratives, and storylines as if they are real. While fearlessly dreaming outside of the box, and most of the time you can never convince them otherwise.

Why? Because it is real to them, which is the true belief of the subconscious mind. The same exact method that I used as a child growing up. A very effective childlike winning principle that I still use today.

I tend to set my mental intentions on dreaming big like a child, and I do this by telling myself the right types of stories. Especially at night before I go to sleep. In a time when the subconscious mind is literally working overtime, and I like to call this.

"The Power of Night Dreaming."

It's the complete opposite of daydreaming.

So, I gradually learned that what I say to myself when no one else is looking is everything, and who I am behind the scenes of my dreams is truly who I am. Meanwhile, I learned that many people are big winners in public, but in secret they are silent failures.

They silently crave attention, acceptance and approval, and in return they become paralyzed by popular belief or the status quo.

I like to call this infirmity, "Losing in Silence."

Now, are you paralyzed by popular belief and the status quo? Or do you delete the need for constant validation, applause and co-signs in order to become your best versions of you?

Well, I hope so.

Because otherwise you would become a cripple as stated in the hit movie "RAY", and the truth is that we are already big winners within our hearts. Yep!

For it is written that whatever I think I am, I am, and it is also written that as a man thinketh in his heart so is he.

I can clearly remember watching a training video by the legendary Floyd Mayweather Jr. and watching him train intensely alongside his personal boxing trainer on YouTube.

He gripped his punching bag tightly as he threw multiple punches. Then to overhear his trainer tell him motivational things like "You're the greatest champ of all times, champ you're the greatest, champ you are #1, champ you're this, and champ you're that etc., only to hear Floyd Mayweather Jr. say back in return,

"Just continue to hold my bag bro, because I don't need you to tell me that. I already know that I'm the greatest, and besides, I tell myself this every day."

Ok, so the moral nuance of this story is that you should never wait for others to tell your story. Because you are the narrator of your own dreams. That's right! So, begin to tell yourself right now that "I am a winner, and I am about to win bigger than I ever have before." Now keep on repeating this winning mantra to yourself until it is internalized with real belief.

CHAPTER 2

My Winners Mindset

MY MIND CONTROL: Which simply means to control the mind, and I often refer to the mind as my very own remote control. Meaning that I am in control of my own mind.

I am persuaded to believe that we are only as strong as our mindset, and when you begin to spell this word backwards you are then left with the amazing phrase "set mind." Which means that we have the authority to set and reset our own minds at will. That's right!

We all have the God-given authority and capacity to dominate the images of our own thoughts, whenever and however we choose.

Now isn't that some great news?

We simply replace the negative images with the positive images, and it all resides in that secret space where winning begins and where winning ends, in the mind.

Because everything rises and falls upon our mindset. Which will always determine whether we win or lose.
If we think like winners, we can begin to live like winners in return. True champions will always find a way to win no matter what! Quite similar to those resilient individuals who never give up until they have reached the threshold of their biggest dreams.

So, I soon learned that the mindset is the only thing that separates us.

The legendary Dani Johnson said that "the only thing that separates the 2 percenters from the 98 percenters in this world is their mindset." Which is simply a mindset that is equipped for winning, and I like to call it, "The Power of Mental Preparation."

Yep!

We must be prepared to win big, and brainwash our minds for achieving massive success, and did you know that you can actually brainwash your mind for major success? Well, yes you can! It is no different than a person being brainwashed by social media and television, and when you begin to say this word "brainwash" backwards it reads "wash brain."

Which means to wash one's brain, and once I became more aware of this mind shift. My life began to soar and elevate beyond boundaries.

Because all growth starts with mental awareness.

MY MENTAL RESPONSIBILITY: Means that I am the one who is solely responsible for the way that I think, and no one else. Which is the accountability for my own thoughts.

Once I began to take full ownership over the narration of my own mind. I eventually gained control over my whole entire life.

Which is why I often use the mantra: "Control my thoughts, Control my life." Ok now you say that with me again, "Control my thoughts, Control my life."

Then I noticed that wherever I was thinking at the time whether it was bad or good, was the result of my own subconscious beliefs, and that I was the one held responsible for my outcomes.

We would often call this "Self-Accountability." Which simply means to always hold oneself accountable.

So, I had to learn that the remote control of my mind was always in my own hands, and that I had the power to reset and set the content of my own thoughts at will.

It's sort of like setting and resetting an alarm clock. You get to set it for whatever time you like, and if you just happen to set it the wrong way at first. You can simply go back and hit reset, and then start the whole process over from the beginning.

Now don't get me wrong, we can't always control everything that happens in our lives, but what we can control is how we think, how we move, and how we respond growing forward. The amazing John C. Maxwell said that,

"We can't control life's difficult moments, but we can choose to make life less difficult. We can't control the negative atmosphere of the world, but we can control the atmosphere of our minds.

Too often we try to choose and control things we cannot. Too seldom we choose to control what we can...our attitude."

Simply put, we are the controllers of our own mental attitudes, and the sad thing is that we often allow others to take that away from us.

We inadvertently become modern day slaves to other people's perceptions and subjective opinions, instead of becoming freethinkers for ourselves. Sure, we look totally free on the surface, but deep down inside we are bound within our own mindsets, and unfortunately most of us become mental slaves to a very compromising society.

BUT HOW DO I RESET AND REPROGRAM MY MIND? THE MENTAL EXERCISE: My whole life was merely a product of the way that I had been viewing myself all along, and how I view myself is how I'll do myself in return.

Then I began to ask myself, "How do I actually reprogram my mind for winning? Or where do I even begin?

Or better yet, what do I really think about myself in private when no one else is looking?

Now, have you ever asked yourself these burning questions before? Well, I'm sure that you have, or why else would you be reading this book?

However, I would like to introduce to you a winning exercise I have been using for many years now.

A very powerful technique that is bound to work for you when it is applied correctly.

I would find the nearest TV remote control and then gaze at all the buttons that were attached to it. To then navigate through the channels and set the timer for a particular show that I was planning to watch later on that day.

Well, the funny thing about this is that I hardly ever watch any television shows these days or any TV for that matter. Lol.

Now, if you have some sort of a remote nearby. Please go to grab it now, and as I said before, I like to think of the mind as my very own TV remote control which is always at my disposal.

So, take a look at the buttons on your remote control to find the off and on button, and then imagine your mind being the remote control for a moment, and your buttons being the means to control all of the mental channels.

The main objective here is to simply become more consciously aware of the fact that you are the one who's in control. Ok, what do you do when there is a toxic TV show playing on the canvases of your brain?

You simply flip through your mental channels until you see something worth watching, and then you enjoy the show.

I like to call this, "The Power of Mental Programming."

The legendary Dr. Stephen R. Covey said, "You are the Programmer."

LOCATING MY THOUGHTS: I learned that in order to properly transform the mind, you have to first locate where you are thinking. Because the mindset needs direction.

I soon discovered that to accurately locate and relocate my thoughts. I would first have to be willing to look into my own mental mirror, and then examine my thoughts from there.

Now this would obviously require some deep soul searching on my part.

Which is where my lifestyle of spiritual meditation and prayer becomes most essential for me. I started to use my daily meditation as a means of locating my own sinking thinking, and boy let me tell you something. It was sinking so deeply at one point that I nearly drowned.

The legendary Lisa Nichols said that "In order to reset your mind to think abundantly you first have to identify where you are currently thinking in scarcity."

In other words, "You have to know where you are thinking in order to avoid where you are sinking."

MY OUTLOOK: Is essentially my optimistic mindset, which is the capacity to always look at things from another angle and perspective, and when you look at this word outlook and begin to say it backwards. You have the popular coin of phrase "look out."

Which is simply the ability to look outside of any situation whether it be good or bad, and then leverage its outcome, and when you say the word outcome backwards you are then left with the phrase "come out."

Meaning that you have the propensity to come out of any struggle no matter how difficult it may be.

For example: when a person is heading towards some oncoming traffic. We typically warn them to do what? Look out!

Then suddenly they began to mind shift, look out, and see that they were heading in the wrong direction all along. Sort of like a mental epiphany if you will.

I can clearly remember having to look outside of my own struggles from time to time, and I must admit it isn't always easy to do. In fact, it is absolutely easier said than done, but at the end of the struggle it is worthwhile.

Because my new outlook became my new freedom, and I am so grateful to God that I am finally able to live my life from the inside out. Rather than trying to live it from the outside in.

FOCUS ON WINNING: When I focus on winning, I tend to win more often, and when I focus on losing, I tend to lose more often. It is just that simple.

I am awakening to the fact that whatever it is that I value the most in my life eventually becomes my focus, and whatever it is that I focus on essentially becomes my reality. Yep!

We all have the common tendency to focus on what we value the most. So, if I place my core values on succeeding for long enough, it will eventually become my focus, and in return succeeding becomes my reality.
Don't get me wrong, we should always value our failures, but our main focus

should always be on winning. Which reminds me of an amazing quote that says,

"When you focus on problems, you will have more problems. When you focus on possibilities, you'll have more opportunities."

The great Tony Robbins said that "You don't experience life; you experience the part of life that you focus on." In other words,

"We become our focus."

THE ENEMY OF MY FOCUS: Back in my high school days, I knew that if I were going to live out my biggest dreams. I would first have to apply some greater discipline, and I knew that in order to reach new milestones and attain the biggest music scholarships. My outside distractions would have to cease once and for all.

Because the greatest enemy to our focus are our distractions. Which are all around us at every moment, and it can be easy to lose our focus and concentration if one would allow it.

This would obviously consist of me staying in some summers in order to practice my crafts
each day, and then sacrificing the majority of my time which is my opportunity. So that I could grow my goals and dreams more effectively.

I truly believe that my focus is my best friend, and my greatest enemy has always been my distractions, but once I conquered those distractions, I gained the necessary fortitude to win massively, and to keep on winning without limits.

CHAPTER 3

The Origin of Creation

CREATING SOMETHING FROM NOTHING: I find that the greatest moments to create is when there is nothing around me. When everything is seemingly null and void.

That's right!

I am well convinced that most of my creative concepts and innovative ideas all came from a space of nothingness at first, and were all born from scratch without any external or tangible means.

For example: when you begin to close your eyes without blinking, what do you typically see? You typically see nothing but pitch black darkness lingering in some black empty space.

However, in the midst of this darkness. I find that it is the perfect opportunity for me to create something bigger and brighter in my life by way of my own thoughts, and my own vivid imagination.

The late great Kobe Bryant said that he would use his really dark moments of isolation, and his fear of failure to create something better in return.

In other words, through much failure, trial, error and reflection, one can learn how to leverage their deepest pains by transforming them into their greatest gains. That's right.

My pain is my gain.

Some of my greatest accomplishments in life were born out of the womb of my darkest struggles and deepest hurts, and I soon learned that the light of my struggle had no true value without the darkness of my pain.

So, I had to comprehend both the light and the darkness simultaneously, and then I started to create some of my greatest work.

However, I truly believe in my heart of hearts that the Creator himself waited until everything was dark before entering into his creative process. The whole earth was without form and void before he ever said,

"Let there be light."

Then the light corresponded immediately and manifested right into its existence, and I gradually started to adopt this same methodology. A three-step creation technique that I still use today, and that is, think light, speak light, and become light.

So, I think it, I speak it, and then I become it by way of its manifestations. Some of us would call this,

"The Law of Correspondence."

See, a few years ago, I had a big company dream along with a big vision and mission to bring more hope into this dark world. Along with some very popular quotes and well-known slogans. Which are,

"Creating hope through arts, business, and entertainment, and "Empowering People Changing Lives"

I can clearly recall having limited resources in the beginning, but I was still willing to grow forward with my big vision, and then we officially released the world-renowned Pure Mission Entertainment. Which all began with a prayer, pen, computer and a few pieces of blank paper.

I can vividly remember creating my own vision board along with creating my own powerful affirmations. I would envision myself launching a global award-winning top-tier company that empowers lives from all over the globe. Something that would be done right in the backyard of our own hometown, city and state.

It was in a rare location where most people leave in order to become ultra-successful, but me and my team were beyond determined to win big anyways. To prosper right where we were.

So, me and my buddy Aaron Emig started to apply these three step winning principles for growth, productivity, and self-development. Which are,

"Crawling, Walking, and Running."

We both discovered that every start up business or project goes through these three stages of crawling, walking, and running at first. Very similar to newborn babies, because the growth is always gradual.

Notice that a newborn baby never comes out of the mother's womb walking and running fast in the beginning.

They typically go through a growth cycle of crawling before they ever start walking and running with speed.

Which is the same process that I often use to grow in every area of my life. The Crawl, Walk, and Run method. I begin crawling first before I walk and then I learn how to walk before I actually start running forward.

For example: I remember watching my beautiful daughter Jazmine attempting to take her very first steps, and I noticed how she would fall only to get right back up to try again, and I like to call this, "The Power of Resilience."

She would keep on trying until she gained the necessary strength in her legs to finally walk forward without falling, and after a few months of continuous effort, she eventually took off running fast with a cute little smile.

I honestly believe that this is the way that we grow our best lives, and it is how we grow in business, in relationships, in wisdom, in knowledge, and in our overall spiritual journey. We crawl, we walk, and then we run forward without ever looking back.

THE POWER OF WORDS: The legendary Bruce Lee went on to say that "Words are energy, and they cast spells, that's why it's called spelling. In other words, my words are very powerful and compelling."

The truth of the matter is that true winners tend to speak like true winners. They typically speak the winner's language, and when I look back over my past life, I immediately get flashbacks about how my toxic words had once trapped me inside of a toxic maze.

That's right!

My toxic words had a great deal to do with my overall lifestyle, and how I spoke about myself had started to sink my winning ship slowly but surely.

I discovered that our words and thoughts are like identical twins that work in unison with one another, and that's when God began to show me the true value of why I should always speak positive affirmations over myself.

He clearly revealed to me that death and life were in the power of the tongue, and if something was about to die, I should always speak life over it.

I used to hear people say all the time that, "Sticks and stones may break my bones, but words will never hurt me."

Well, that's not necessarily true, because I found out that not only can words hurt you, but words can also cripple your capacity to dream big and even worse kill your self-esteem as a person if you allow it.

"Words can either heal you or kill you."

Which reminds me of a beautiful young teen by the name of Isabell, who took her own life because of this same tragedy. There were some very harsh words spoken to her across social media and at school, and unfortunately those dark powerful words played a very significant role in her demise. RIP

However, once I woke up to the fact that my words became my reality. My speech started to drastically change for the better. It started to gradually change the trajectory of my whole entire life, and I'm talking right from the inside out all because of my winning words.

I can clearly remember all those dark days of being caught up in what we often call "The Trap." When I would say to the homies, "don't get used to seeing me right here", because I am about to leave this life alone once and for all, and I repeated this winning mantra every single day along with my winning intentions at every opportunity.

It was all done by faith, and I was basically calling those things that were not as if they already were, and you know what folks? It actually worked! It all came to pass in real time, and this became one of my greatest secret weapons for true freedom.

SELF-INVENTORY: simply means to do inventory on oneself. So, we must inspect ourselves to know ourselves, and we must know ourselves in order to grow ourselves. This is what we call, winner's introspection.

Now let me say that first part again: "Self-Inventory simply means to do inventory on oneself." So, we must inspect ourselves in order to know ourselves, and we must know ourselves in order to grow ourselves.

Some of the most burning questions that I tend to ask myself everyday are, what value have you been creating and inventing in your life Willie J.?

Have you been creating any inventions of value for other people to grow and learn from? Or have you been reinventing yourself for wealth and riches lately?

See, my main objective here is to simply help you to become more consciously aware of this winning concept and principle called self-inventory.
Then if you take the last three letters off the word inventory you have "invent." Which simply means to produce or create something new for the first time, and I believe that we are all inventors to some degree.

Because we are always creating something new with our lifestyles each and every day.

Do you remember when I mentioned in the previous chapter that we execute this by the way that we think, move, speak and react? Or when I talked about saying the word "Lifestyle" backwards in order to style our lives properly?

Yep, we must take full notice of what we have been creating in our lives every day. This is done to clearly locate and measure up all of our hidden blind spots, and to consistently focus on ourselves and not others. Because when you stay focused on growing yourself, you will have a greater chance of knowing yourself.

However, there is a time to create and then there is a time to do inventory on what's been created. Even God himself rested on the seventh day to gaze at his master piece called creation. To merely reflect on what He had just invented, and to see that his genius was absolute perfection.

Then we have the business store owner and the entrepreneur who are required to do daily inventory on all of their products, goods and services. Something that is typically done as a means of scaling and charting the company's overall growth and progress.

With that being said: I have officially vowed to always do self-inventory on myself in the same manner, and that is to always analyze my good, bad, pretty and ugly. Because my first and most important business in life is always me, myself and I.

Ok now let me say that once again. I said that "my first and most important business in life is always me, myself, and I."

LEVERAGING MY RESOURCES: We must leverage every moment whether it be good or bad, and when we are creating, I learned that we should always leverage our own resources, and to never despise the days of small beginnings.

Because small beginnings can eventually lead to big endings over a period of time.

Now let me say that one again. I said that "small beginnings can eventually lead to big endings over a period of time." So, use what you got!

Some of the greatest inventors in history started out small at first with only a concept and a witty idea. For instance: The legendary Thomas Edison had very little resources in the beginning of his masterful creation of the light bulb and sound recordings, and his first resources were only the resources of his thoughts, which he consistently used for its development.

So, don't you ever be afraid to begin a big dream or big project small. Just be consistent each day in what you are trying to build and create.

Because consistency will multiply over time. Or as John C. Maxwell would often say, "Consistency Compounds."

Now start creating that masterpiece of yours today. It is quite similar to creating a hit record from scratch, and in the beginning all you may have is the beat.

Along with a few creative chords and some beautiful words to a melody.

Then from that point on, you begin to build up the song from there. Which can essentially lead to you creating a catchy chorus along with some very memorable verses.

Or when you're writing a bestselling book. You typically start off with some great footnotes, bullet points, and a unique title with a thesis at first. Success usually begins with very little.

CHAPTER 4

I'm Growing To Win

THE POWER OF PREPARATION: Is essentially the preparation of power which simply means that there is power in preparation. It is the blueprint to fulfilling our biggest endeavors. So, let us always prepare for the power that we desire to possess.

I was finally starting to figure out that everyone in life wants to be great at something, but very few people are willing to grow in the designated areas that it takes to get there.

Now sure, we all desire some sort of greatness, but most times we want that greatness without having to properly prepare for it. We want to go without having to grow.

Alright, now let me say that one again. I said that "we want to go without having to grow."

Eventually, I learned over time that I must grow before I can go, and I must train before I can gain the necessary momentum growing forward. This is why me and my dream team believe in what we like to call,

"Preparation before Destination" or "Preparation before Elevation"

The legend John C. Maxwell said that "Preparation positions people correctly, and it is often the separation between winning and losing." In other words, big wins will always mandate big preparation. It gives us the necessary momentum and synergy to succeed.

See, we are all preparing for something more, and from the very moment that we are born into this dark world we begin our journey to unforetold destinations which will always require preparation.

Even before our day starts, we typically go through patterns of preparations first, and oftentimes we go through the processes of taking care of our personal hygiene, washing up, showering, and analyzing our best apparel to put on that day.

Now, have you ever noticed when we are traveling far distances, we pack up our bags, check on our oil, fill up on gas and check our tire pressure levels for safe arrival?

Or before taking a flight, the pilot is usually required to check on all the air pressures, the weight of the plane, and the weight of the bags before ever taking off? Well, sure you have.

Which reminds me of a very popular mantra that I like to live by today and that is,

"Stay light for the flight."

That's right. We must stay light for this flight called life, because sometimes we travel with too much excess baggage on our planes.

BUT WHAT AM I PREPARING FOR: I started to discern that my preparation will always need direction and strategy. It is the GPS for my growth. Preparation requires strategy.

The big winning questions that I tend to ask myself are: Where am I preparing to grow next? Am I preparing for the best possible outcomes? Or am I preparing for the worst possible scenarios? Am I living my life by design or am I living it by default.

After all, how can I arrive at my greatest destination in life if I don't have a game plan on how to get there? I would soon discover that there is a right way to prepare for a thing, and there is also a wrong way.

I find that the majority of people in life have no clue of what they're preparing for. Too often, they find themselves scattered all over the place with no sense of direction. Merely growing in circles and growing nowhere fast.

However, I began to finally comprehend through much trial, error, and reflection that:
"You can't grow what you don't know, and you have to know where you're growing now in order to know where you're growing later."

I am reminded of the great Peter Druckee who said that "If you can't measure it you can't improve it."

Which became the same approach that I used for practicing my instruments before gigs, or the way that I prepared my vocals before attempting to record them in the studio. I would repeatedly rehearse the material well enough to articulate it gracefully when it was time to execute, and guess what? I never needed any paper.

The same winning principle that I often use to scale my businesses, career, relationships, and my overall lifestyle, and I like to call it "Scaling My Life."

IT TAKES DISCIPLINE TO BE A WINNER: Self-Discipline is the key component to having massive growth and success, and without it we can't keep growing. The word discipline derives from the word student. So, I must always remain a student of the game.

I knew that in order to be truly successful at achieving anything. I would have to first possess self-discipline. Which simply means to discipline oneself.

It is the hidden recipe for our infinite growth, and we must be willing to consistently expand our current successes to live out our future successes.

That's right, I like to view my success as a big plant, because you can always do it better. Know it better and grow it better.

You know those great leaders and great achievers that I mentioned earlier? They could not have become that legendary without having self-discipline.

They had to ultimately sacrifice their time, their energy, their money, and even certain relationships to achieve that level of greatness. It is totally inevitable.

However, I noticed that the more that I became a student of this game called life, the more that I grew exponentially, and I finally came to the conclusion that massive success would not happen for me overnight. It would actually take some time.

It would require me grinding it out each day nonstop with a lot of blood, sweat and tears, which is the very reason why I would often find myself practicing each and every day. Even when I didn't feel like it. Yep!

When I didn't feel like exercising I did it anyway, when I didn't feel like reading, I did it anyway, when I didn't feel like praying, I did it anyway, and when I didn't feel like growing in knowledge, wisdom, and understanding. I still did it anyway.

The legendary boxing champ Mike Tyson said that "Discipline is doing what you hate to do but doing it like you love it."

Soon, I discovered that when you keep on doing a thing over and over again. You eventually learn to like it and love it over a period of time. So, once again folks, it's all about that mind over matter.

RELEASING MY WINNING POTENTIAL: Simply means to have the potential to win. Because anything is possible when you have the confidence to take immediate consistent actions.

I perceive that we all have some sort of God-given winning potential buried inside of us. Just waiting to be expressed, released and exposed to the universe.

That untapped possibility of becoming great one day, and soaring high above everyone else's expectations. The possibility of becoming a great beacon of hope and light for all of humanity to see.

However, before we can officially release this type of winning potential. We must first be willing to look inside of ourselves, and to see where the true potential is, and we do this by practicing, shedding, and always striving to be better. We must stretch ourselves without stressing ourselves.

That's right, I said that "We must stretch ourselves without stressing ourselves." Or how can we ever know what is possible?

Potential is the possibility of being and becoming something that hasn't materialized yet. It is the hidden possibility of what is to come, and the hope of what is not seen.

Meanwhile, I learned that Discipline + Consistency= Potential, and the more potential that you have, the more possibilities you have in return, and to waste one's potential is to literally waste the possibility.

See, the main idea here is to always get better and grow a little bit more each day, and that's even if it means growing in tiny segments and progressing one baby step at a time.

For it is still better for me to grow a little bit at a time, than to not grow at all.

Which reminds me of another great quote by my mentor John C. Maxwell that says,

"Small disciplines repeated with consistency everyday lead to great achievements gained slowly over time."

In other words, grow yourself gradually brick by brick, layer by layer, inch by inch, and then watch your winning potential begin to soar right out of the roof. Now let's grow together!

MOMENTS AND MOMENTUM: Our growth needs momentum and our momentum needs growth. When we maximize our moments, we begin to create momentum. Which is why each moment of my life I intentionally set the bar high for my day by starting off with what I like to call my "first fruits".

A very blessed moment and time where I set my spiritual intentions first thing in the morning before doing anything else.

With the idea of no social media, no phone calls, no meetings and no food until a certain part of the day.

Now why do I do this?

It is simply to gain more control over the overall flow and energy of my day. In a time when my preparation meets my destinations in a most unexpected way.

This actually gives me the type of fortitude to persevere. Which comes from leveraging every moment and transmuting those moments into something greater over time, and when you take the "um" off the word momentum you are left with the word "moment." So, I like to call it,

"Moments and Momentum."

The more that I take out the proper time to prepare myself. The more that I gain a competitive edge to win big in everything that I do. That's right.

"Because moments create momentum and momentum creates moments"

No different than the momentum that drives me and my company every day into deeper depths and higher heights of success. We literally maximize our winning potential by maximizing every moment.

John C. Maxwell said that "Often the only difference between winning and losing is momentum."

Then I noticed that the greatest teams are usually the teams who can leverage their moments and momentum the best, and I'm talking about at all times and in all climates. Very symbolic to a statement made by the legendary Anne Sweeney who quoted that,

"Our future is only limited by our commitment to keep the momentum."

In other words, when you gain the proper momentum in your life, keep it and sustain it until you see the winning results that you are looking for. We must commit to our momentum, because our momentum will always need commitment.

Notice, before a winning team ever reaches that championship status or dream, they usually go over winning strategies and winning techniques at first.

No different than a dominant athlete or a musician who is propelled to greatness. When he or she begins to prepare themselves with intense training, intense techniques and vigorous exercises.

Something that is typically done in order to gain and sustain the best momentum possible for when it is game time.

Because winning is all about preparation, adaptability, and being able to shift gears at any given moment when it is necessary, and I'm talking about being able to shift gears in any atmosphere, and in any weather.

The real reason why a good team can start off winning big in the first half of a game with all the momentum, and then suddenly lose it all in the second half to lose the contest.

Well, undoubtedly it was because the winning team had allowed the losing team to gradually steal and take away all their momentum. Which means to have leverage.

Hence it is the same reason why the legendary basketball coach Phil Jackson won so many NBA Championship titles.

Or why the legends Kobe Bryant and Michael Jordan won so many back-to-back rings as pioneers of the game. Along with their amazing teammates.

It is the exact same reason why the great Tom Brady and Coach Belichick won so many NFL Super Bowl titles year after year.

Right along with the legendary Patrick Mohomes and Kansas City Chiefs head coach Andy Ried doing the same thing. Now why is that again? It is because they all learned how to "Leverage every moment to their advantage, whether it be good or bad under pressure."

They all mastered having great momentum.

GROWING IN A WINNING ENVIRONMENT: A growth environment is a winning environment, and a winning environment is a growth environment.

The one thing that I had to change along with changing my mental environment was transforming the environment in which I lived. The very environment where I had lived most of my entire life.

So, I began to ask myself some very important questions: Is this environment that I'm living in conducive for the personal growth that I'm trying to attain? Or is it actually holding me back?

While it remains to be true that it is very possible for one to alter his or her mindset in any atmosphere.

However, I would also discover that to reach a certain plateau of greatness and success, my external domain would have to change as well. Meaning the environment of my friends, the environment of my family, the environment of my peers, and the environment of my whole inner circle.

In the amazing book "The 15 Laws of Growth " John C. Maxwell stated that "I believe at some point during every person's lifetime there comes a need to change environments in order to grow."

WINNING RELATIONSHIPS: Are simply the relationships that help you to win big in life. Do you have the types of relationships that help you to win big? Or do you have the types of relationships that cause you to fail miserably.

I liken this word relationship to a ship that is either sailing towards more greatness or sailing towards more failure, and when you begin to take the word "relation" off this word relationship you are then left with the word "ship."

Because relationships will either sail you forward or sink you deeper. Which will essentially determine how anchored you are.

So, I envision a ship that is full of people with various relations and relatable qualities such as compatibility, vision, character, purpose, spirituality, and the overall mindset.

It is where I begin to genuinely ask myself: are these relations with the people that are currently on my ship helping me to sail forward in life? Or is it sinking me deeper into more failure and defeat? Because the most frustrating thing in life is to be involved in relationships that are growing nowhere fast. That's right! I said growing nowhere fast.

CHAPTER 5

Winning Habits

CRAVINGS AND APPETITES: The reality is that we are all driven and fueled by our daily appetites and cravings, but what are they exactly?

Are my daily cravings and appetites driving me to grow better, or are they driving me to grow worse? That is the real question here, and this is when I discovered that my everyday habits can eventually determine the overall quality of my life.

After doing some very intense research. I learned that this word habit means having a regular tendency or a practice of doing something, and it is no secret that we are all products of what we practice each day.

That's right. We are all products of our choices, routines, and everyday habits.

However, down through the years I started to comprehend that every habit of mine had an appetite, and it could only be starved or fed by its repetition. Yep.

Repetition is not just the art of learning, but it is also the food for our habits. Why?

Because the more that we do a thing with consistency, it eventually becomes a part of who we are. It organically becomes a part of our whole anatomy, character, and DNA.

Now as I mentioned before, our consistency multiplies over time, and it will gradually increase our appetites and cravings. That is why Consistency+Practice+Appetites and Cravings= Habits.

Ok, let me say that again, "Consistency +Practice+Appetites and Cravings=Habits."

Meaning that whenever we practice a thing with consistency. It increases the appetite for wanting more, and this is how habits are developed and formed.

We typically eat from the fruits of whatever we rehearse and entertain each day, and once again. The only way to transform a habit is to repeatedly starve its desire, appetite, and cravings. Because anything that starves for long enough, it eventually dies, and this is where fasting and prayer comes into play for me.

MY ADDICTIONS: I finally concluded that all my addictions in life were not so bad after all. I just had to become more addicted to the right sources.

Yep, I realize now that any habit can become an addiction over time, and that is whether the addiction is good or bad.

Because our habits don't discriminate, but rather blossom like a newborn flower that blooms in the early morning of spring.

Now why is that again? How did it essentially become an addiction?

Well, it is simply because all addictions are connected to the wombs of our daily choices, decisions, and routine habits. In short, our habits become addictions, and our addictions become habits.

You know, all those toxic addictions that we often suppress and hide deep down inside of our haughty pride? Or sealed deeply in that dark place where only you and God can see them?

However, back in the day I recall developing some very questionable habits and addictions of my own, and those habits nearly killed me to say the least.

I found myself drowning in the pools of my very own addictions, and I was literally starting to suffocate fast. So much so that I could barely breathe at times.

Yep, I was literally starting to knock loudly upon death's front door, and I almost got an answer several times over.

I'm talking about a series of near-death experiences here, and I just thank God for transforming my entire life, and for him saving my wandering soul."

I finally came to grips with the fact that if my habits had not changed, my life wouldn't change much either. For one's life to truly change their lifestyle must change first.

For example: I can remember smoking cigarettes many years ago as a bad habit, along with having some excessive drinking habits at times, and the more that I would feed into those bad habits, they eventually grew into my deepest addictions. But once I began to starve the appetite and cravings of those bad habits, they gradually vanished once and for all, and to never return.

WINNING HABITS: I sincerely believe that our daily habits in life will always determine the totality of our future, and eventually determine whether we win or lose.

Which reminds me of another great quote made by John C. Maxwell that says,

"We don't rise to the level of our goals; we fall to the level of our habits."

In other words, I knew that if I were to become a big winner in life. I would first have to practice like a bigger winner, and then develop the appetite for big winning habits.

I would need to force feed my motivation, and then starve out my bad habit of procrastinating. I would have to stretch myself in order to grow myself, and I like to call it stretching myself without stressing myself.

That's right!

We have to be willing to stretch ourselves without stressing ourselves in order to grow further.

It is no different than a bodybuilder having to stretch their muscles before attempting to build them up, and I soon learned the way that they stretch them determines the way that they will grow.

With that being said, I advocate that a winner's future success is fully determined by his or her winning habits. Which reminds me of another great quote made by the legendary Jack Canfield who said that,

"Your habits will determine your future."

In other words when my habits change, my future changes right along with it, and only then can I begin to think better, do better, feel better, and live better overall.

"We are what we practice."

Then someone asked me the burning question one day: "Willie J., what is your practice in life? Then I replied, "My practice in life is always to win big in the end." I practice winning big in my mind, winning big in my heart, winning big in my business, winning big in my relationships, and winning big in my soul. I always practice to win, though I fall short of it sometimes.

GETTING RID OF MY TOXIC THINKING: Our toxic thinking will always poison the potential of our biggest dreams. So, I had to gradually pivot my thoughts and start thinking differently in order to live differently.

Once again, my daily first fruits meditations have always played an intricate role in controlling the mental movies playing inside the theaters of my mind.

It has undoubtedly been the most effective way for me to set the right tone for my day. Quite similar to a mental detox if you will, which simply means detoxing the mind.

In those very dark moments when my toxic thinking had almost gotten the best of me. I had to remember that my toxic thinking could lead me into living a toxic lifestyle.

Because we become what we think, and our thoughts are like sperm cells and seeds that impregnate the subconscious mind.

The legendary James Allen said in his classic book "As a man Thinketh" that,

"Every aspect of a man springs from the hidden seeds of his thoughts and that a man is literally what he thinks."

That's right, we are like spiritual farmers who sow seeds into our hearts and minds each and every day. Then we all reap what we sow.

With that being said: I had to have somewhat of a mental miscarriage in my mind to birth a new one. Which meant no more toxic thinking for Willie J.

Yep, I had to take the word" brainwash" and say it backwards over and over again in order to wash my brain properly. So, I started to detox my mindset for massive success.

LEAVING MY TOXIC RELATIONSHIPS BEHIND: I find that having very healthy relationships will always enhance one's chances of winning big in life, but I also found out that the unhealthy ones can cause you to lose big time.

Let's just say that I learned a multitude of hard lessons from being in the wrong relationships. As I suddenly found myself entangled in some very toxic alliances which nearly killed me.

I was engaged in some very dangerous entanglements, and I am just so blessed and grateful to still be alive.

My illegal partnerships almost destroyed me, my dreams and my purpose simultaneously.

So, I began to learn that the true value of my life had solely depended upon the quality of my relationships, and that it could eventually determine the outcome of my tomorrow. Because relationships will either lift you up or take you back down deeper into your past.

The legendary Les Brown said that,

"You have got to upgrade your relationships and continue to evaluate them, and make sure they are an asset to you and not a liability."

In shorter terms, relationships will either make you or break you in the end game, so please be aware.

Now, I was fully persuaded to weed out any and everyone who had ever posed a real threat to me living out my God-given potential, purpose and dreams, and it didn't matter who you were, you could've been my family or my best friend.

At the end of the day, if you were a toxic individual that didn't mean me well. You would automatically get canceled out of my life all in the name of love.
That's right, I still love you though, but unfortunately, I must love you from a distance.

Tony Robbins said that "Who we spend time with is who we become."

Well, my most personal mantra for relationships is, "If we cannot grow together, we cannot go together", and it is a golden rule that I apply to all forms of relationships.

After all, the whole point of any relationship is to add true value and quality to one another, right?

I AM WHAT I EAT: So, I always eat to win. That's right, I am what I eat, and I always strive to eat with a particular purpose in mind. I am no longer eating to just survive, but I am simply eating to thrive.

During my exciting journey to health and wellness. I gradually discovered that my health was really my wealth. You know the popular saying "Health is Wealth." Well, it's true.

It is when we become the very foods that we store into our physical bodies each day. Because the food that we eat is not just food, but it is also spiritual.

Yep, food is energy.

Then I began to notice that when my eating lifestyle changed, the whole trajectory of my life changed as well, and I began to feel more energized to do the things that I was most passionate about.

Along with having more momentum to fulfill my life's purpose and calling. I guess you can call this a mental epiphany as well. Because my mind became much clearer, sharper, and stronger than it was before.

Suddenly, I could remember just about anything once my eating habits changed, and my brain was finally able to store unlimited information.

My whole entire life was literally starting to transform all because of the way I was eating. Which is why we become what we eat, and this can also be applied to the eating of knowledge and the eating of wisdom.

I am now reminded of another great quote from the bible that says, "My people are destroyed for lack of knowledge."

Now why is that?

It is simply because knowledge is symbiotic to having food, and if we don't feed our mind, we can't grow any further.

This is why I love reading and absorbing powerful content, because man shall not live by bread alone but by every word that comes from up above.

I like to call it my soul food, or my food for the soul. Yelp, our food affects the soul. Which is our mind, our will, and our emotions.

So, the magical questions are, "What types of foods have you been eating lately?

"Is it good food or is it bad food? Is it rich food or is it poor food?" Now you decide.

THE POWER OF MY NOW: Now is the only moment that is guaranteed to us. Even our future depends on it.

We actually have to live in the present in order to experience the future. When you take the word "now" and begin to spell it backwards, you are then left with the amazing word "won."

Meaning that if you are actively taking immediate actions right now you have already "won" half of the great battles ahead. Because being present wins championships. That's right!

NOW is always the best time, and it is the most powerful moment in the universe. There are no promises for the future of tomorrow.

Other than the pure fact that we are all appointed to eventually die one day. So, I like to call this beautiful gift from God, my present. Which reminds me of an amazing quote by the legendary Eleanor Roosevelt that says,

"Yesterday is history, Tomorrow is a mystery, Today is a gift. That is why we call it the present."

See, oftentimes our greatest deception in life is feeling as if we still have enough time to transform a thing. We subconsciously assume that our next moment is automatic, and that our future is always on autopilot.

Well, news flash folks, it isn't!

I soon discovered that not only is now my most precious gift from God, but it is also my golden opportunity to grow and learn more as I grow forward.

That's right, my time is my opportunity, and to waste my time is to literally waste my opportunity.

Now who can afford to waste that? Not me, not you, not anybody simply because the power of my now will always determine the power of my tomorrow.

Ok, now let me say that again, "The power of my now will always determine the power of my tomorrow."

So, I can no longer afford to allow the enemy of time who is my "procrastination" to creep into my world and steal away my most precious opportunities to succeed. You know that golden opportunity to be better than you were yesterday? Right!

Which is why I strive to grow everyday like it is my last, because I may not get the chance to grow again tomorrow.

This is why we must always take immediate actions, to gain traction, and then gain attraction. It is the three step process for winning big, and if you notice in all of the three steps, the word "action" is mentioned and spelled out three times.

Pretty dope, right?

CHANGING MY ATTITUDE ABOUT ME: How I feel about me is all that really matters, not what other people think. It is always me versus me.

Have you ever taken the time out to really listen to things that you say to yourself each day? Or ever took notice of your most personal dialogue sessions about you?

Ok, what is your clear view about you when no one else is looking? Or did you know that how you view yourself is how you will eventually view others?

That's right. How you view yourself is how you will view others, and how you view others is how you will view life, which can eventually determine how you are viewed in the lenses of very significant people.

I am now reminded of an amazing quote from the legendary Zig Ziglar who said that "Your attitude, not your aptitude will determine your altitude."

In other words, if you think upward for long enough, you will begin to grow upward, and if you think downward for long enough you will surely begin to grow downward, and that is when I discovered that keeping a positive winning attitude can carry an average person a very long way.

It can sometimes qualify you for positions of power that you may not be qualified for on paper. Now did you know that?

People of influence will suddenly begin to overlook other great resumes just to collaborate with you, all because of your positive winning attitude and mindset.

Simply because possessing good energy can always make up the difference between a person winning and losing. A good attitude is everything.

THE POWER OF GRATITUDE: When you take the "gr" off of the word gratitude you are then left with the word "attitude." Which will always determine the overflow of your abundance.

That's right. Gratitude is true abundance, and true abundance is gratitude, and I began to notice that the more grateful that I became in my life, the more abundant I became in return. It was as if the windows of heaven were finally starting to pour out an abundance of blessings that I didn't have room enough to receive.

Now why was that? It was merely because I had chosen to be more grateful in my heart rather than to be bitter about the things that I didn't have, and I started to discover that an ungrateful heart will only lead to having more things to be ungrateful for.

It is very similar to the quote made by the legendary Lisa Nichols who said that "Energy grows where Energy goes." Which is so true. Meaning that wherever we store our energy, that energy will eventually reciprocate and compound.

Very similar to the compound effect.

Meanwhile, my life was starting to show me the other side of the coin, and it was all because of my gratitude shift to become more grateful for all the things that I currently possess.

Ok, now imagine that for a moment, and I mean imagine being grateful in all climates too, whether it be sunshine, rain, sleet, or the icy snow. Then making a vow to become more grateful for every waking moment, and to never complain again about the things that you don't have.

Well, you may be asking yourself right now. Why shouldn't I complain about things Willie J.? My answer is because you already have everything living on the inside of you!

LEARNING TO ENJOY THE JOURNEY: I had to eventually start focusing more on the journey rather than the destinations. Which is when I learned how to detach myself from certain outcomes.

I am now reminded of a great trip that me and some of my best buddies took back in the day to Boston, Massachusetts. We were on our way to the legendary Berkeley School of Music. Which was orchestrated and spearheaded by their beautiful mother who goes by the name of Helen P. Harden. RIP

A very beautiful soul who always showed me and the fellas unwavering love and support for our musical endeavors, who had simply come long to oversee the whole process of Theo moving into his brand-new college dorm room on campus.

However, I ended up taking a completely different route and was soon offered a major music scholarship from one of Aretha Franklin's percussionists, who went by the name of Professor Bolen. A legendary professor who taught me the true meaning of the word specificity.

So, we sat down at the table to eat up our lunch that day, and Mrs. Harden began to drop a very powerful gem on me, and that was "Enjoy the Journey."

She said that "It's not always going to be easy to get where you are trying to be in this life, Willie. However, you are headed to some amazing places young man, but just remember this one thing, and that is,

"Enjoy the Journey."

I was only 18 years old at the time, and I realize now that this had a great deal to do with me making the proper mind shifts in my life. Which totally transformed the way that I had been perceiving my trials and tribulations.

What she was essentially saying is, don't just enjoy the good moments. Learn how to enjoy and appreciate the growth that comes from the struggles as well.

Enjoy the process!

I HAVE TO LISTEN, LEARN, AND GROW: To listen is to learn, and to learn is to grow. This life is all about listening, learning, and growing into your best version.

Well, I can honestly admit that I was not always the greatest listener in the class, and I can clearly see now that it was simply because I didn't understand its true value at the time. I would often confuse hearing someone out with actually listening to the heartbeat of their content.

So, I found myself speaking up way too soon. Which caused me to cough up unnecessary information and advice prematurely.

Boy, I just couldn't wait to shoot out those bullets of my own biased opinions, but with a few minor adjustments all of that changed over a period of time through much trial, error, and reflection.

Once I became a better listener, I became a better person and a better leader all in the same breath. A brand-new focus was born, and even my grades started to skyrocket beyond everyone else's expectations of me, even my own.

Right along with my comprehension skills increasing once I got rid of all the toxic noise pollution. Because I learned that who and what we listen to will determine what we know and how we grow. The great Les Brown said that "what you tune into is who you turn into."

In other words, we must listen to the right voices to make the right choices, and my firm belief is that every mentor needs a mentor, and every coach needs a coach in order to keep growing forward

Now what I would like you to do is to ask yourself: Who and what am I listening to each day?

THE POWER OF SILENCE: Most people believe that emotional aggression and loud noise compensates for having true power. However, I discovered that the true power is in solitude and stillness.

The power of silence is the silence of power. Which simply means that there is power in silence, and some things are better left unsaid, and what's understood doesn't always have to be said.

Right? It is a winning posture that took me a good minute to figure out, but once I grasped it. I became way more effective as a leader than ever before. Because silence became my super power.

That's right, most individuals typically speak with the motive to only be heard, and to only prove a certain intellectual plight, and most of
the time it is only to sound impressive before others.

Meanwhile, as a motivational speaker, life coach and teacher myself, I discerned that it is way more beneficial to leave the audience blessed rather than impressed. Because impressed people don't always change and prosper, but blessed people do.

Which is something that I absorbed from speaking in pulpits, banquet dinners, graduations, leadership seminars, masterminds, and global workshop summits around the world.

Now with that being said, what I discerned is that sometimes your silence can speak much louder than your words. Simply because it gives you more time to think, more time to analyze, more time to empathize, and more time to respond appropriately to the matter at hand.

It gives you more perspective power, and more of a competitive edge when you are able to remain calm, poised, and resolved under very intense circumstances. Yep!

I liken this winning concept to the art of making the proper chess moves. Which is essentially the ability to always think before we act.

Because when you overreact you take the blind risk of losing all your composure and all your momentum. Less is always more in my book, and no I don't mean this book guys. Lol

However, by way of much prayer and meditation. I have learned to become way more conservative with my energy under intense pressure. Meaning that I tend to choose my battles more wisely these days.

Now, please do understand that it wasn't always this way, and to be quite honest I was the very opposite. I was very quick tempered and would pop off at any given moment if I felt threatened but thank God for true transformation and emotional intelligence.

I am now reminded of some amazing quotes made by the great King Solomon who said,

"There is a time to speak and a time to keep silent" along with another great quote that says, "Even fools are thought wise if they keep silent and discerning if they hold their tongues.

But what does silence really mean?
Silence is simply the absence of all sound and noise. So, we must always be willing to find that quiet place within the still waters of our own mindset.

Our peace is priceless, and you can't go online or to any convenient store to purchase it. It isn't for sale.

MY PEACE OF MIND: True peace is not the absence of war, trials, and tribulations but it is rather the absence of all worry. So, we must learn to protect and preserve our God-given peace at all times, no matter what.

One of my favorite hit records by the very talented Lauryn Hill is entitled "I gotta find peace of mind." The kind of peace of mind that we all long for even when we're not fully aware of it.

Yep. Especially in a season with so much deep-rooted hate, and not enough love on display.

That inner calm that we all so desperately desire in a time of brutal warfare, but unfortunately most of us fail to ever receive it. Which is an indication that our perception of reality is somehow being distracted by all the outside noise.

I eventually learned that peace of mind is all about perception, and perception is all about reality, and the real secret to having peace of mind is being at peace with those things that we cannot control. That's right. When we try to control and force outcomes, we gradually lose our peace. So, "control what you can control."

Ok, remember when I mentioned in Chapter 2 that we can't always control the things that happen in our lives? Other than how we choose to respond and react to them?

Well, that is still very true.

It is always about being able to "Grow with the Flow" and leveraging every moment to our full advantage whether it be good or bad.

To be able to block out the very next second by taking no thought for tomorrow and trusting in the mere fact that tomorrow will always take care of the things of itself.

What I began to realize is that there is so much peace and potency in just being present, and not worrying about anything else outside of that.

So once I started to focus more on the present moments rather than my past history. My peace of mind soon became one of my greatest weapons in disguise, and I finally possessed a successful peace of mind.

Napoleon Hill said that "You have not found success unless you are at peace with yourself and all others."

Which is the type of peace that comes from God and introspection. The kind of peace that surpasses all logical understanding.

Now for a brief mental exercise: Take a quick moment to jot down all the things and the people that bring you joy and peace. Then erase all of those things and people that bring you sadness, heartbreak, and anxiety. Only focus on peace.

SIMPLIFY TO AMPLIFY, KEEP IT SIMPLE: I discovered that there is real power in practicality, and I am continuously learning how to just keep things simple in a very complex world.

Have you ever noticed how we can sometimes complicate the most simplistic matters in life? Or how can we actually make things much harder than they ought to be?

We oftentimes make the difficult more difficult, and the complex more complex, and we typically complicate the complicated without even realizing it.

However, what I have come to notice is that simplicity is key, for it is the hidden power to self-discovery and the undercover solution to all tough tasks.

Yea, you heard me right, I said that "simplicity is key, for it is the hidden power to self-discovery and the undercover solution to all tough tasks."

When you attempt to make a complex matter easier, then it becomes easier in return, and it really doesn't matter how complex or complicated the matter is.

I like to call it my mind over matter, because it's all about perspective, and taking a simpler approach to life's most difficult challenges and doing it gracefully in the most impactful and practical manner.

Now with that being said, I really do believe that simplification breeds amplification, and as you begin to apply these winning principles and concepts to your life.

It is extremely important to remain calm while doing so. Because the more that you relax with the information by way of simplicity, it then becomes way more achievable and easier to reciprocate.

Then I noticed that when we are truly relaxed in our minds. We tend to think better, believe better, do better, and achieve better.

Which is the same exact method and approach that I use when practicing my crafts. Or when it comes to me recording, singing, speaking, and performing on the big stage.

When you intentionally make a thing simple for long enough, it then becomes more simplistic by nature.

On the contrary, if you believe something to be very difficult for long enough, it will in return become more difficult by nature. It is "The Law of Perspective."

It is really that simple. Now, try this mind shift for at least three days or more and watch what happens to your growth.

THE POWER OF LAUGHTER: Over a certain period of time my laughter became my superpower, and my superpower became my laughter. It became the cure and medicine for all forms of sadness and depression.

I started to absorb that my healing was wrapped up inside of my ability to laugh. Which reminds me of another great quote by the legendary King Solomon who said that "Laughter is good for the soul." Meaning that it is good for the mind, the will, and the emotional well-being of the man.

It can apparently cure mental health, deep depression, stress and sometimes even cure cancerous diseases based on some medical reports.

Now imagine for a moment, laughter being some sort of healing medicine and cure for pain, or some antidote for our deepest miseries and disappointments.

I know, it's kind of hard to believe right? Especially when you're right in the thick of whatever you're struggling with at the moment.

Well, it's true though, because I found out that one of the cleverest ways to deal with any form of hurt, trauma, or pain is to find some sort of laughter inside of it, and I'm talking right in the middle of that storm, in the middle of that rain, and in the middle of those unfortunate hurricanes that present themselves so unexpectedly. Rest in Peace to all the Hurricane victims.

It can literally become a person's greatest secret weapon, which reminds me of a great quote made by the legendary Mark Twain who said that "Laughter is the greatest weapon we have and we, as humans, use it the least."

In other words, we should complain a lot less and laugh a whole lot more. Even if it requires you watching your favorite TV show or that funny sitcom that brings you pure laughter. Laugh out loud until your low frequency becomes a high one lol.

That's right, laughter can suddenly change the climate around you, and it can organically heal your mental well-being. It will shift your focus on the good things that are happening around you rather than the bad things.

So, what I started to witness, and notice was that a lot of my success and winning in life had greatly depended upon my capacity to laugh.

The legendary Andrew Carnegie said that "There is little success where there is little laughter."

CHAPTER 6

My Drive to Win (Driven)

DRIVING TO SUCCESS: I gradually learned that true winners are always ambitious and self-driven, and they tend to never wait for others to drive them forward. Because they drive themselves. The legendary Gloria Steinem said that "Leaders, we do what we see, not what we're told.

It was then when I discerned that true winners are go-getters by nature. They always take responsibility for their own motivation.

Have you ever noticed when you have your own set of keys to go and drive as you please that you never ask anyone? Well, I most certainly have, but why is that exactly?

It is because the permission is already granted, and furthermore why would you have to wait for someone else to approve of you driving your own vehicle? Right?

You simply take action by getting inside of your vehicle, starting up that engine, and then you take complete control over your own steering wheel while driving forward. Now, what if we were able to take this same mental approach in driving our own dreams forward? How much more powerful would we be?

Well, I believe that we would become unstoppable forces to be reckoned with, and being self-driven would become second nature.

See, many times we wait for others to Uber us to our designated areas in life. Only to realize that we already have the keys to our own vehicles, along with having our own tools and resources.

We have the gas, we have the engine, we have the oil, we have the mirrors, and we also have the tires to drive forward with balance.

For quite some time now, my deepest motivation has always been to win big, and to keep on winning big for as long as I can remember.

To consistently live my life with intentionality and purpose and like to call it "My Purpose Driven Mindset." Via a mindset that is driven by a particular purpose.

However, I believe that we are all self-driven to some extent, and that we are all inspired and motivated by something or someone each and every day.

From the very moment that we are blessed to wake up every morning. We are driven by our daily tasks, our daily goals, our daily ambitions, and by what we see, touch, hear, taste and smell. We are deeply motivated by all our five senses.

Yep!

So, the real questions would be, what is your deepest motivation in life? Do you just wait for others to inspire you? Or do you motivate and drive yourself?

One secret that I discovered is that, when you become more purpose driven, and remain driven by a particular purpose, you will always remain driven.

That's right!

Because your drive is constantly being fueled by its purpose. Which is our passion and our why. It is my why that keeps me driven, and it will always drive me to unlimited success.

MY INNER DRIVE: Our inner drive comes from within, and when you begin to say it backwards and take the "er" off of the word inner, you are then left with "drive inn." Yep!

In that secret place where our inner drive lives, and in every room, there is a belief, a dream, a purpose, a vision, a calling, a goal, a project, and a business, and in the other rooms there's patience, resilience, faith, fear, failure, pain and love.

Now, if there is one thing that I have learned over the years, it is that my big dreams and goals will not drive themselves.

No sir!

There has to be a driver in the seat and guess who that driver is? Well, that's none other than you and me, my friend. We must be the drivers of our own dreams and destinies.

It is always about taking immediate actions, gaining traction, and then gaining the necessary attraction to grow forward.

Because our goals and dreams all have wheels, and they must be driven by the driver, and the owner of that vehicle is you!

The incredible Les Brown once said that,

"Wanting something is not enough, you must hunger for it, and your motivation must be compelling in order to overcome the obstacles that will invariably come your way."

HOW TO BECOME MORE MOTIVATED: Motivation comes from self-accountability, and then taking immediate massive actions each day. It stems from having a purpose driven mindset, and always driving oneself to the next level of success.

People will often ask me these questions: "So Willie J, how does one become more motivated with the necessary drive and motivation to succeed? Or how do I possess the proper motivation to commit to all my daily goals, tasks, and dreams?"

I simply replied that, "motivation comes from a person doing a particular thing for a particular purpose over and over again," and then getting the best possible results from it.

It ultimately comes from me taking consistent immediate actions each day, because the more that you practice a thing with results, the more motivation you get for practicing it again.

See, it all goes right back to the three-step winning process that I mentioned earlier, and that's taking actions, gaining traction, and then gaining the necessary attractions to grow forward.

The amazing Kobe Bryant said that "he gained more motivation and inspiration from the results of his practicing hard every day."

In other words, the greater the practice results, the greater the motivation, and the greater the motivation, the greater the elevation.

That's right, no motivation, no elevation. Now imagine an airplane or a jet trying to elevate without any gas or fuel in it? How pointless would that be?

So, I noticed that whenever I would practice on my craft, with a motive for getting better results. It would literally inspire me to come back again, but with a greater propensity.

Basically, my motivation for practicing hard was fueled by the awareness of my new growth. I simply leverage my progress to gain more progress in return. It is all about allowing your progress to motivate you, and then it essentially becomes your personal fuel to succeed in a more dynamic manner.

I believe that we are all like vehicles that need fuel and oil in order to function forward, and without the proper fuel in our tanks, we lose our capabilities of driving the distance. Why? Simply because our gas levels will always determine the distance of how far we can travel.

Ok, let me say that once again "Our gas levels will always determine the distance of how far we can travel."

So, with that being said, I learned that a person is only as strong as their motivation, and a person's motivation eventually becomes their will power. In those sacred areas where our true intentions and desires live, and when a person doesn't have the will power to win. They simply don't have the motivation to win, and without the proper motivation to win. Unfortunately, you just can't win.

But what does this word motivation mean in context? Wikipedia said that motivation is an internal state that propels individuals to goal-directed behavior. Simply put, without the proper motivation you will not grow very far in life.

Now, for a quick self-evaluation exercise: I would like for you to take a moment to look at yourself in a mirror, and then begin to ask yourself this simple question, and that is, am I a self-motivated individual?

BELIEVING IN YOURSELF: Self-belief is a key ingredient for having long-lasting success, and it is the hidden recipe for authentic leadership. Especially with Imposters Syndrome on the rise.

All winners must have a great sense of self-belief, which simply means to believe in oneself. So, if you ever dreamed of being great one day. The first step is to believe, and if your goal is to eventually become massively successful in your field of expertise and knowledge. You must first believe that it is all possible. We have to believe that we can do it before we can do it.

Now don't get me wrong, it is extremely important for us to believe in God, but we must also believe in ourselves. Then I gradually learned that to believe in God is to believe in myself, and when I doubt myself, I am indirectly doubting God. Now isn't that refreshing to know?

Because every good and perfect gift comes from up above.

However, I do understand that it takes real courage for one to truly believe in themselves, and it can be downright challenging at times, but we still must believe.

It is the gasoline to all our dreams, and a dream that is without belief is simply a dream that is without fuel.

As I mentioned before, we are all products of our own mindsets and belief systems, and we cannot grow any further than what we can believe about ourselves.

We are what we believe.

Hence is the reason why so many of us fail at starting and finishing up our biggest projects.

Why?

It is simply because we don't believe in ourselves enough to follow through with them, and the sad part about it is that we will sometimes believe big for other people more than we will ourselves. Then some of us will even believe in a slot machine first. Wow!

John C. Maxwell said that "You will never be able to bet on yourself unless you believe in yourself." In other words, if you believe in yourself then you should bet on yourself, and did you know that the greatest enemy to our beliefs is our "disbelief"?

Yep, a very low frequency called "disbelief." Which can essentially kill our biggest dreams.

To make it more plain, we receive what we believe about ourselves, but the magical questions are. What do you believe about you, and how do you truly identify with yourself?

Do you believe that you can win big, and never stop winning? Or do you view yourself as an inadequate failure?

What I started to find out is that when you truly believe in yourself for long enough, other people with influence will eventually believe in you too.

The legendary Dr. Myles Monroe said that "When you believe in your dream and vision, then it begins to attract its own resources."

TRUSTING THE PROCESS: Is really about trusting the journey, and sometimes the journey can look scary, but it is very necessary. So, what I learned is that God's timing and alignment is always perfect. Yep! It is absolute perfection.

In everything that we do there is a process before its progression, and there is always a test before the actual promotion. Then I discovered that my progress in life is always determined by the quality of my process.

In other words, "No process, No progress."

See, many times we desire the progress of having massive success without having to go through the necessary nuances.

We want the big promotions without having to take the big test. We want the biggest trophies without having to grind hard for it, but we have to grind before we can shine. That's right,

"We have to grind before we shine."

Which was the moment when I realized that even pure gold goes through the process of fire before it is finalized. So, what makes us any different?

Before a student can receive their high school diploma or college degree. They are always mandated to go through the process of taking some courses first, and if they fail to pass those particular courses, they simply cannot graduate.

However, we must go through the necessary trenches no matter how difficult they are. Which will literally give true value to our success. That's right, our process will always give true value to our progress. Otherwise, how can we know the true worth of the blessings?

Now, let's talk about this word process in commentary for a second. It is a series of actions or steps taken to achieve a particular end.

Which essentially means that there will always be a series of action steps taken to attain and gain true success.

It will oftentimes require a strong belief system. Along with having some unwavering faith that every step of the way is leading to something greater.

When we think of the words progress and success. We should automatically think of the words: belief, preparation, timing, alignment, and patience.

Which is where most of us give up, and throw in the towel. Because we expect it to always be easy when it is not.

See, sometimes we fail to realize that anything worth having in this life will take time, effort, and great struggle.

The amazing pioneer Fredrick Douglas said that "If there is no struggle there is no Progress." In other words, it is our struggle that gives birth to our progress, which are the sperm cells to all our dreams.

CHAPTER 7

Failing To Win

WINNING FROM MY MISTAKES: I fervently believe that in order to understand winning. We must first understand failure. Which is why me and failure became best friends over time.

I had to eventually come to grips with the fact that in this life some mistakes were going to be made unintentionally, and that those mistakes were only here to help me grow into my next best version of me.

So, I started to recognize that some of the biggest winners in life were also some of the biggest failures at one point, and they were all just human beings like me.

Well, I can clearly recall making a lot of costly mistakes in my past life, but through much trial, error, reflection, and correction as my buddy Richard Mover would say. I was finally able to capitalize and transmute them into my biggest gains.

However, I learned that on my best or worse days I am still a work in progress, because there is always room for improvement.

After all, King Solomon said that "A just man can fall seven times but he will rise again" and it is the very reason why we should always continue to, "Leverage every moment whether they be good or bad."

Because failure is just an opportunity to win, and it is a golden opportunity to conquer life beyond all its boundaries. It is how we grow with the flow.

We fail at first and then we learn how to win later from that same failure. Which is no different than a championship caliber team who may have failed at the beginning of their season but ended up winning the whole entire finals.

Now, what made up the difference between this team losing and winning? Well, it was simply their ability to remain confident, and their ability to remain present. Along with their ability to remain resilient under some very intense pressures, and when it mattered the most, they showed up. That's right.

They made the hard adjustments, and eventually learned how to do as John C. Maxwell would say,

"Fail Forward."

See, once I learned how to properly fail forward without complaining. Winning became my new habit, and then I learned how to think better, do better, be better, see better, and believe better for my life.

OVERCOMING THE FEAR OF FAILURE: The fear of failure is simply having the fear of imperfection, and I soon discovered that my greatest fear in life was always to be perfect, and as a perfectionist, my efforts for perfection became my greatest fear.

Unfortunately, most people's greatest fear in life is the possibility of failing miserably at something, the fear of not winning, the fear of not growing, and the fear of not knowing what is going to happen next.

However, life is all about taking big risks, and embracing the unknown, and then being courageous enough to do it even when we're feeling afraid. That's right, when it scares you beyond your wits, do it anyway, and at least you can say that you gave it your best shot.

So only be courageous!

Which reminds me of a great quote made by the great Vince Lombardi who said that, "Winners Never Quit and Quitters Never Win." In other words, you only lose when you stop trying.

Can you imagine if Kobe Bryant had quit trying to win an NBA title after shooting all of those air balls in the finals of that year? Where would his amazing legacy be right now had he given up?

He had to courageously face the risk of being ridiculed, the risk of being criticized, the risk of being shamed, and the risk of taking the overall blame for the Lakers losing the championship that year, and I'm talking right in the midst of millions of viewers.

Instead, he chose to get over himself, make the adjustments, conquer his fears of failure, and then come right back in the following season to win three back-to-back championship titles along with his amazing teammates.

So, whenever I find myself failing in a particular area in life, I tend to get excited about it and accept the challenges head on.

Because I know deep down inside that this is a golden opportunity to grow further, win bigger, and become better than I was yesterday.
It is all about growing with the flow day by day, month by month, year by year, and leveraging every moment of our greatest fears.

EVERYONE MAKES MISTAKES: Sometimes, we forget to remember that human beings aren't flawless at all, and that we are all subject to making some mistakes at times.

When I really think about it, my darkest moments were when I would constantly beat up on myself for not being perfect, and for sometimes falling a little short of my greatest efforts. Only to find out that no one was perfect at anything, and this even applied to the biggest winners in life.

Because winning isn't perfect, and I discovered that even when we know a thing, we don't always know it the way that we should.

Yep, you can always know it better than you did yesterday. "For there is always room for improvement, no matter how great you are."

We all fall short of our delusional versions of perfection and flawlessness, and we all drop the ball sometimes, but we can also pick it back up again to score the game winning touchdown.

Because perfect winners in this life don't exist, and we are all prone to making some mistakes from time to time. See, we all need failure in our lives, or how can we properly value winning?

We must first understand the value of failing before we can understand the value of winning. Our failures are the gateway to winning, and our errors are simply the blueprints to our success. Which kind of reminds me of a great quote by John C. Maxwell that says,

"Without failure there could be no achievement and when you fall be sure to pick something up." In other words, no failure, no progress, no losses, no wins.

MY BEST IS ALWAYS GOOD ENOUGH: Which is why I never settle for anything less than giving it my best shot. Because my best is always my best version of me.

The only thing that we can do in this life is give it our best shot, and allow God to do the rest, and in the end, we still win because we genuinely gave it all that we got. Yelp, I said that "The only thing we can do in this life is give it our best, and allow God to do the rest, and in the end, we still win because we genuinely gave it all that we got."

At any rate, giving it your best shot takes a great deal of courage, and I would soon discover that the only way that I can lose is if I don't try. Which is a constant reminder for me to always give it my best no matter what.

That's right. My best is always good enough, but I would often feel the very opposite in those days, and it really didn't matter if I was winning or losing. I just couldn't see the big picture of it all.

So, I started to gradually drown in the pools of my own insecurities and inadequacies, and I found myself constantly trying to give what I didn't have to give. Then I heard a wise man say that "You can't give what you don't have, so just give it your best shot."

SETTING MY INTENTIONS: When I set my motives and intentions upon winning, I typically win big in the end no matter what.

However, I still find myself falling a little short of the bar at times, but just because I fall a little short of the bar, doesn't mean that I shouldn't aim to win.

Because the ultimate motive is always to win in the end game. Then once I became more aware of this winner's mindset, my mistakes and failures started to minimize. Yep!

My wins were finally starting to overshadow my losses for a change, and I was really beginning to grow with the flow, and the more that I set my intentions upon winning big, the more that I won big. Some experts would call this,

"The Law of Attraction."

Now, let's talk about the meaning of the word intentions for a moment. According to the Merriam Webster Dictionary, it is something that one hopes or intends to accomplish and it means to set up a goal or a plan. In other words, my goal and game plan should always be to win big in the end. It is the key frequency for our greatest victories.

Our winning intentions are similar to road maps that can essentially lead to many destinations of great successes and achievements.

Les Brown said that "Your goals are the real road maps that guide you and show you what is possible for your life."

So, when we set up our goals for winning, we get more winning potential in return, and then I noticed that some of the biggest winners in life all had winning intentions, and that's even amid making some of their biggest mistakes.

However, we should always be intentional with our growth, because growth is not accidental. It must be done on purpose. We must always live a purpose-driven lifestyle.

Which is simply a lifestyle that is driven by a particular purpose, and once I figured this out. The whole trajectory of my livelihood changed for the better.

It is the why behind my what, and my why is what drives me forward every day, and you know what else I found out?

I found out that the more that we game plan our growth. Is the more intentional our growth becomes.

Chapter 8

Faith Over Fear

MY SUBCONSCIOUS FAITH: Which is the hidden belief of the unseen, and the subliminal faith that we use from day to day on autopilot. Now, has it ever occurred to you that we all walk by blind faith without even realizing it?

We breathe in God's fresh air each day just knowing that we will get another chance to breathe it again, and we organically assume that we'll have the precious opportunity to inhale and exhale without ever thinking about it.

Yep!

Subconsciously, we believe in the hope of the unseen, and we courageously anticipate our next greatest moments. We assume that it will always be there waiting for us. Which is why I tend to never take my next breath for granted.

For example: I can remember losing a dear friend and classmate who recently died in his sleep without having any previous illnesses, and I'm sure that he didn't believe for one second on the clock that he would die in his sleep on the day that he did.

He obviously had the great expectations of waking up the next day. Just like anyone else would, but he didn't. RIP

However, I discovered that every move that we make and every breath that we take is an act of faith. From the very moment that we set our alarm clocks to wake up on the next day with game plans, it is an act of our subconscious faith.

Now, why am I sharing this amazing theory with you?

Well, I'll tell you why. It is simply to heighten your awareness, and to help you become more consciously aware of the subconscious faith that you are already utilizing every day. So that you can charge it, recharge it, activate it and amplify it for greater gains.

For another example: When we start up our vehicles to go and drive to certain destinations throughout the day. We sincerely believe and have the confidence that we are going to arrive there just fine, and in a timely manner all in one piece, and even the animal's journey subconsciously by faith not knowing if it is their last day.

MY FAITH IS NOW: Now faith is the only kind of faith that wins, and when we think of the word faith, we should always think in terms of the present moment.

Now!

Ok, let's talk about this word faith in context for a minute. The Dictionary.com says that faith means to have confidence or trust in a person or something.

The Merriam Webster dictionary says that faith means to have a firm belief in something for which there is no proof. Which is basically believing in the unseen. Then the bible says that faith is the substance of things hoped for and the evidence of things not seen, and I have learned that anything that can be done now in the unseen is literally done by faith. That's right, if you can do it now in advance, that is faith on display my friend.

Because faith always deals with the now-ness of time, and when you begin to spell the word now backwards it leaves you with the word "won." Do you recall me mentioning that earlier?

Well, I'm sure that you do.
When we begin to take immediate massive actions now. We are actually taking a leap of faith, and this is what releases miracles.

That is simply what faith is, it is the knowingness that you have already won the great battle before it begins, and it is the capacity to win the battle in your heart before it ever starts.

Yep, it literally means to live your life from the inside out. Which is the only way that a person can truly walk by faith and not by sight. "You have to see it all from within"

BUT HOW DO I GET MORE FAITH: Once again, I believe that true faith is born from the inside out, and that it is the evidence of things not seen, but how do we acquire more of it?

Well, for starters, it is written that "Faith comes by hearing and hearing by the Word of God." So, I learned that faith comes from the words that we speak and listen to each day. Meaning that if you hear those words for long enough. You will eventually start to believe them over time.

That's right!

The very reason why it is extremely important for us to monitor what we hear and speak. Because our words are very impressionable, and our mind cannot tell the difference.

The amazing Napoleon Hill said that "Faith is a state of mind that may be induced or created by affirmation or repeated instructions to the subconscious mind."

In other terms, whatever the mind can perceive and believe by way of words, it will actually conceive.

Or when you begin to tell yourself over and over again that I am a winner, and doubt not in your heart. Eventually, the subconscious mind will process the data and give you more faith and confidence to believe just that.

Simply put, the more that we repeat a thing. The more that we believe in a thing, the more that we believe a thing, the more that we conceive a thing.

"We conceive what we believe."

For instance: I have a mental mirror technique that I like to use with my clients from time to time, and I would like to sincerely introduce it to you as well.
It simply requires that you look into your own mirror each day while quoting

winning mantras and affirmations to yourself, and then to continue repeating these affirmations out loud every day until you start to believe them. Ok, now let's go!

FAITH DOES NOT PROCRASTINATE: When you sincerely believe in something, and love what you are doing. You will always have proactive engagement, and that's even during being afraid. Yep!

When I think of the word faith, I automatically think of taking immediate massive actions along with taking some immediate massive risks, and to me faith is always a big risk worth taking, but in order to do this most effectively.

I would have to ultimately get rid of the woulda, coulda, shoulda syndrome, and then take some immediate massive actions towards my dreams.

After all, faith without works is dead, and our faith should always have legs and a heartbeat that does not procrastinate or hesitate under pressure.

Which sort of reminds me of a great quote made by the legendary coach Pat Riley who said that, "shoulda, coulda, and woulda won't get it done."

Or my Uncle Tony who quoted to me many years ago that "woulda, shoulda, and coulda ain't never helped nobody."

In other words, we must execute our faith, and that's even in the midst of being terrified at first. We have to do it afraid, and you know the old saying,

"You will never know, unless you try."

Now, don't get me wrong, it takes real genuine courage to walk by faith and not by sight, and in most cases our procrastination is an indication that we are afraid. It is the hidden reason behind most people failing to take big risks in their lives. Because they fear the possibility of what could go wrong.

Simply put, they fear failure.

However, the only way to truly overcome the fear of failure is with our confidence. Our success will always mandate courage and confidence over fear.

So, whatever it is that you truly desire to do in life. Do it right now by faith!

THE ENEMIES OF MY FAITH: Are simply my fears, my doubts, and my disbelief, and it took many years to figure out that we were all at war with one another.

Through much trial, error and reflection. I started to learn that one of the greatest enemies to my faith was my f.e.a.r. Which simply means false evidence appearing real. That's right, when you break that word "f.e.a.r" down it simply means false evidence appearing real. Or false evidence altering reality.

Meaning that my fear is simply an illusion of what is not present. It is only a figment of my imagination. It is the worry of unborn promises, and it is the anxiety of a made-up world that doesn't exist, and in most cases, we fear that which we cannot see.

We fear premature trials, we fear premature tribulations, we fear premature circumstances, we fear premature lack, and we fear premature catastrophes before they ever occur.

So, I learned that this is the main handicap that cripples our faith with limitations, but fear not.
Because there is absolutely nothing to fear. A wise man once said that "the only thing we have to fear is fear itself."

We have to be brave, we have to be bold, and we have to be courageous, even when we are unsure. Because this is the only way to conquer our fears.

John C. Maxwell said that "To conquer fear, you have to feel the fear and take action anyway."

That's right, we have to face it, embrace it, and then erase it. Which is the only way to leverage our fears.

MY GUITAR CENTER FAITH: Never be afraid of doing what hasn't been done yet, and always accept the big challenge to make history.

I vividly remember being asked to headline and run my very first drum concert clinic at the legendary Guitar Center, which was a huge honor considering that some of the world's greatest musicians, artists and talents had previously performed there.

It was literally like a childhood dream of mine unfolding right before my eyes around the same timeframe that I had been featured in two of the world's biggest drum magazines. Both in Modern Drummer and Drum Magazine simultaneously, and boy I was so beyond excited about this opportunity. Yep!

Because the magazines had featured some of my biggest childhood heroes, and to be mentioned in the same breath with these legends was nothing short of euphoric. It was a freaking miracle to say the least, "Glory Hallelujah."

However, this major press would eventually grab the attention of one of the biggest Guitar Centers in our city and state at the time, but there was one catch. They told me that I only had two weeks to promote this big event. Which typically took up to two months or more in advance to promote.

"Uh Oh, here we go again."

Most people would have panicked in this scenario, but this was my golden opportunity to either rise with courage and confidence or fold under the pressures of fear and doubt.

This was my golden opportunity to take the "ure" off of the word pressure again, and to start pressing forward with some unwavering faith, and I like to call this,

"Growing with the Flow."
That's right, I chose to grow with the flow, and shortly afterwards I was randomly

asked a few logical questions by the two store managers who had invited me.

"So, Willie J., do you really think that you can pull this event off with such short notice dude? Because no one has ever done this before?"

"I mean, can you really get the people to show up with only two weeks of promotion?"

Then I paused and hesitated for a brief moment and looked right into the face of my own fears and answered them both boldly and said, "Yes I can." As a matter of fact, I know that it will be a very big hit, just wait and see."

This is what I like to call, "Calling those things that are not, as though they already were."

It was all a great leap of faith, and surely all the odds were stacked up against me without a doubt, but my faith was much stronger than the odds that were stacked up against me.

The stakes were very high now, and my word, my name, my integrity, and my reputation were all on the line in a major way, and I just had to deliver the goods.

So, I immediately began to meditate day and night with some of the most intense visualization techniques ever, so much so that I dreamt about the whole event being crowded in my sleep. Which was only a few days away.

Wow!

My subconscious faith started to elevate and soar out of the roof, despite me being a little challenged with fear, but I thank God that I was able to eventually overcome it.

Meanwhile, I began to take some immediate massive actions growing forward by heading out to the print shop to print out some of my own flyers, and shortly afterwards I hired my very own street team to pass them out with me.

We all came together to strategically place flyers upon any and everything that was moving in sight, upon every vehicle, upon every business, and then we started to hand them out to every person that we encountered.

A great maneuver that I learned from my Dad who promoted successful concerts when I was a little boy.

I just had to go hard in the paint and give it my absolute best shot, and then allow God to do the rest in return. "I had to put my money where my mouth was." Because there was no turning back now, and it was either go big or go back home defeated.

Now, one of the biggest events of my life is finally here, and the anticipation was really starting to intensify. So, I pulled up to the Guitar Center with my fellow musician buddies Theo, and Ben. Just to witness a parking lot filled up with crowds of people gathered from all over the world. With a reach that went as far as Pakistan.

Wow, I was so blown away by the big turn out, and so were the managers.

I mean, there were so many people at the event that night that they had to place it upon their big screens outside of the building for people to watch.

Man, it really worked!

Placing my faith beyond my fears when it mattered the most, and the dopest part about it is that my mom, my dad, my friends and my family got to witness it all.

I'm telling you for a fact that anything is possible, if you can just believe it. That's right, believe it, conceive it and achieve it.

MY MOUNTAIN MOVING FAITH: I gradually learned that mustard seed faith can essentially move big mountains, and there is no mountain so big that it cannot be removed.

No sir!

In this life we all have big mountains to face in a variety of ways. We face big mountains in our finances, we face big mountains in our businesses, we face big mountains in our relationships, and we face big mountains in our everyday lives.

For as long as I can remember my life has always been filled with big mountains, and eventually I learned that I was the one solely responsible for moving them.

Many times, we tend to wait for others to move our big mountains for us, and we fail to realize that we have been given the God-given authority to move them ourselves.

That's right!

The same mistake that I made many years ago, but once I discovered that whosoever shall speak unto this mountain to be removed and cast into the sea, and doubt not in his heart. Can have whatever he or she says. The whole trajectory of my life began to drastically change for the better.

Yep!

When the big mountains would appear, I would simply speak against it with faith, and the real truth of the matter is that we have to believe that the mountain is going to be removed before it actually moves.

For a quick example: When I was previously told by the Guitar Center managers that I had only two weeks to promote one of the biggest concert clinics of my life. I immediately thought of a big mountain being removed, and I knew that I would have to be the one to speak against it.

After all, this was a major event that normally took up to two months or more to promote, but I was up for the big challenge, and anytime that we think of the word faith. We should automatically think of the word challenge. Because our faith will always face temporary challenges.

Which is why we take the word "outlook" and begin to spell it backwards in order to "look out" in faith.

Ok, now notice my response to them, when I was asked if I could pull off this monumental event with such short notice. When I would answer them back "yes I can" right in the face of fear.

Or when I stated that not only will I pull off this big event. It will also be jammed packed with crowds of people from all over the world.

So, what was I really doing in all essence? I was simply speaking unto my biggest mountain with unwavering faith, and surely enough we watched this big mountain be removed and casted into the sea.

CHAPTER 9

Forgiveness Is Freedom, Bitterness Is Bondage

THE LIBERTY OF FORGIVENESS: Literally means that we have to truly forgive in order to be free, to be free in our hearts, to be free in our minds, to be free in our souls, and to be free in every genre of life.

To be totally honest, there is no challenge in being unforgiving towards someone. It takes no real effort at all. In fact, it is downright easy to do, but the real challenge is having to forgive that person.

Yep!

Having to forgive the same individuals who may have wronged you for no apparent reason at all. Which can be very difficult at times, but also very rewarding in terms of freedom.

I'm talking about freedom in success, freedom in business, freedom in relationships, freedom in peace, freedom in ministry, freedom in love, freedom in joy, freedom in our minds and freedom in our eternal souls.

However, I know that this is easier said than done, but the struggle is totally worth it.

There is just something so powerful about forgiving others amid their wrong doings. It is as if you are controlling the dynamics of your own freedom from the inside out.

I like to call it, being more conservative with my energy, because it consumes a great deal of energy harboring unforgiveness. It can be downright draining beyond words.

Oh, trust me, I know! I guess it's safe to say that I have been there and done that already, and on the day that I finally learned how to properly forgive and let go. I also learned how to become more liberated and freer.

Forgiveness is power, and it is the hidden remote control to our freedom, but what does this word really mean?

According to the Merriam-Webster's Dictionary, forgiveness means to pardon or cease to feel resentment against an offender. It is the hidden resentment aimed towards an individual who may have offended you, and if ever you need to know if you have truly forgiven them.

Check for the resentment, and begin to ask yourself these questions: Do I still feel any sort of resentment when their names are mentioned? Or do I still feel peace, love and freedom inside?

"To forgive, or not to forgive, that is the question?"

So, I started to discern that you don't necessarily forgive others for them, you forgive them for yourself. Meaning that it is for your own personal benefit.

That's right!

This is the only way to stay elevated and light for the flight. We must keep the wind beneath our wounded wings, and be lean enough to fly anywhere, any place, and at any given moment. Now let go of that past hurt and start flying!

BITTERNESS IS BONDAGE: A bitter heart will only lead to having a bitter vision, and it will essentially sabotage the overflow of our biggest dreams. Right after doing some extensive research, I learned that the word bitterness means having a feeling of antagonism, hostility, or resentfulness towards another person or thing.
Simply put, my bitterness is bondage and my forgiveness is freedom.

Which reminds me of some very dark moments in my past. During a dark time when I had allowed my own suppressed bitterness to get the best of me. You know the type of bitterness that no one else can see? Or the kind of bitterness that hides behind superficial smiles, and artificial hugs?

I'm sure that you get the picture here.

However, I found myself drowning in the rivers of my own bitterness, and I noticed that I was only hurting me, myself, and I.

That's right, slowly but surely my life started to take a downward spiral, and my bitter ways of thinking gradually became my mental imprisonment.

Then I finally discovered that bitter hearted people made bitter hearted decisions, and that bitter thoughts could eventually lead to bitter actions and bitter outcomes. Because we still become what we think, and it is nearly impossible to be genuinely happy and free when deep rooted bitterness is dominant.

Bitterness is bondage, and it is the thief of joy, and the thief of peace.

LOSING MY BITTER MINDSET: A bitter mindset will only keep you down, and it will gradually prevent you from reaching your greatest potential. Trust me, I know.

It was when my beautiful mother and grandmother passed away just one year apart from breast cancer. Which caused me to become a little bitter with God momentarily.

Yep!

Suddenly, I began to drown in the darkest pools of my own mental despair, and I was in desperate need of a new mind shift.

When you begin to spell this word backwards you are then left with the phrase "shift mind."

Do you recall me saying that earlier? Meaning that we must shift our minds in the right directions even when we are hurting deep inside, but how exactly?

For starters, I would have to acknowledge my true emotions, and then face the music of those conflicting feelings head on, and after that find an area of forgiveness in my heart towards God and the whole situation.

I would have to gradually heal.

After all, those loved ones were not suffering here any longer, and they were finally resting in eternal peace. Which was the moment when my mind shift became my most valuable asset.

It was all about having a newborn perspective and being able to finally look outside of my darkest problems no matter how dark they were. Do you remember in Chapter 2, when I talked about the winner's mindset being the ultimate key to a person's success in life?

Or when I mentioned a person only being as strong as his or her mindset, and when you begin to spell this word backwards you are then left with the phrase "set mind."

Yep, I'm sure that you do.

In other words, we must take full control and ownership over our own bitter way of thinking, and the truth of the matter is that I really needed to learn how to genuinely forgive others, and to finally let go of the pain.

That's right!
Now, don't get me wrong, this doesn't mean that I have to allow these same negative people back into my inner circle. It just simply means that I no longer have any resentment in my heart towards them.

The amazing Lisa Nichols said that "Forgiveness doesn't mean you are letting the other person off the hook or pardoning their behavior." It does not mean that what happened didn't hurt you, that's not it at all." Forgiveness is committing to not being consumed by anger, frustration or hurt.

So, I eventually learned how to let go, release, and forgive, and it is something that I like to call, "The power of release" or "The power of forgiveness." Which is how I practice forgiving others to remain free. I practice releasing myself so that I can free myself of any negative energies growing forward.

FORGIVING MYSELF TO BE FREE: In order to forgive others, we must first learn how to forgive ourselves, so I had to learn how to face it, embrace it and then erase it.

Remember that?

Ok, now say that with me one more time, "Face it, Embrace it, and then Erase it." It was a massive blessing to discover that once I learned how to forgive myself. I would soon learn how to forgive others as well, and to truly forgive myself, I would first have to pardon my own failures and mistakes.

After all, my failures made me who I am today.

The legendary Brian Tracy said that "You must absolutely forgive yourself for every silly, senseless, wicked, brainless, thoughtless or cruel thing you have ever done or said."

This must be done to soar high, and to release one's winning potential into the universe, and I like to call this winning principle, "The Power of Self-Forgiveness," which simply means to forgive oneself.

Ok, now begin to ask yourself this question, and I need you to be totally honest. "Do I truly forgive myself for all the wrong that I've committed, both unintentional and intentional?

Because sometimes the very reason why we are unable to soar in our lives is simply because we are too weighted down with self-guilt, self-blame, self-shame and unforgiveness towards our own personal defects.

That's right!

We consistently rehearse the memories of our own past failures, past mistakes, past pains, and past shortcomings. So much so that it gives us a sense of unworthiness towards ourselves.

You must know that you deserve to win before you can actually win, and you have to know that you deserve to be free before you can actually be free.

So, forgive yourself right now, and finally become liberated, and always remember that the Creator loves you, which is why you should too.

Your self-worth is everything!

I CHOOSE TO LOVE: True love is never forced; it is a choice and an action word. It is freely given out a heart of forgiveness.

Forgiveness is a choice, and there is always an option to forgive or not to forgive. The choice is solely up to you. It is the master key to all true freedom, abundance and love.

But what is love exactly?

Love is simply a strong positive feeling or affection for another person or thing. It is the capacity to let go of all bitterness, and it is the most powerful frequency in the universe.

The legendary Dr. Martin Luther King Jr. said that "Love is the only force capable of turning an enemy into a friend."

Which is simply Agape Love.

The only force capable of providing true power, true healing, true character, and true transformation from the inside out.

However, in order to understand this level of love and forgiveness, one must first understand the dynamics of unforgiveness and hate. Which is the root of all division, but love is unity.

Yep!

Over a period of time, I started to recognize that it feels way better to love than to hate.

So, I chose to live with my L.O.H. which stands for,

"Love, Over, Hate."

LOVE WILL ALWAYS WIN IN THE END: True love will always conquer hate. Which is why I choose to love? For me to love is to win, and for me to win is to love. See, most of our failures in life are due to a lack of love.

CHAPTER 10

Growing Under Pressure

SUNSHINE WITH THE RAIN: We all need some sunshine in our lives, but we also need the rain in order to grow. I guess you can call this, "My Growing Pains."

As I sit here game-planning and writing out the content for this tenth chapter. It is officially Mother's Day. A bittersweet holiday where I find myself having to take the "ure" off of the word pressure.

Which spells out the word "press" in return, meaning that I must press forward while leveraging my deepest hurts and deepest pains, and I'm talking about transmuting my deepest frustrations into some of my most monumental moments.

"Pain is Gain."

In due season, I was finally able to celebrate all those precious moments that me and my mom shared, and I eventually discerned how to shift my whole perspective. With God's help of course.

Now, let's talk about this winning concept of taking the "ure" off of the word pressure for a brief moment, and where it actually stems from. For as long as I can remember my life has been under some sort of intense pressure, and if there weren't any form of pressure, I wouldn't know what to do with myself, literally.

It has always been sunshine with the rain. So much so that I had to eventually write a song about it. So I wrote a very heartfelt record that turned out to be an international hit record which charted extremely high on the European Top 200 Indie Music Charts, and we were all so beyond excited about it to say the least.

A big shout to Stephen Wrench for pushing the record overseas.

However, before I could even record this global anthem in the studio with one of my best engineers and clients. I would end up receiving one of the worst phone calls of my entire life, and to make matters even worse, I was already vomiting under some intense pressure.

Then right in the midst of that pressure, we received a very tragic phone call that my cousin Lamar had been found dead in the back seat of his car, and immediately I began to break down with immense tears beyond words.
Woe!

Shortly afterwards, Ken, who was one of my engineer buddies, sent me his sincere condolences and asked me if I had needed to reschedule our recording session for another day. Then I can remember taking a deep breath along with a deep sigh to gently reply.

"Wait bro, let me go and pray about this matter some more, and then I will get right back to you."

Meanwhile, I went on to pray fervently about the whole situation, and then I heard a still small voice inside of me saying "now go and take the "ure" off of this word pressure, and then press forward to the studio and record this big record."

This inner voice revealed to me that something amazing was about to happen, but that was only if I would be willing to leverage this most difficult moment and turn it into my greatest gain.

Which reminds me of another great quote made by the very gifted Kobe Bryant that said, "Everything negative-pressure, challenges-is all an opportunity for me to rise."

That's right, it was a golden opportunity for me to rise high, and immediately I called back Ken and Arthur Flash Johnson to tell them both that we would continue with the studio session, and that something very amazing was going to happen as a result of it, and you know what? That is exactly what happened. Something amazing!

A big shout out to Jeff Anderson for letting us use the studio. Yep!

As bad as I needed the sunshine in my life, I also needed the raindrops as well. I needed the rain in order to grow further with my life, and I gradually learned that the raindrops, which symbolizes my "growing pains", had just as much value and significance as the sunshine. If not more.

It is quite similar to a plant or a tree that is in need of both the sunlight and the rain in order to grow effectively.

So, I liken myself to a living plant or a living tree that is firmly planted by the rivers of living water. Which is simply how we continue to grow with the flow.

For instance: two months prior to my mom passing away from breast cancer. I would also receive my first book publishing deal and distribution deal through Ingram books, and just one year later, my beautiful Grandmother passed away from breast cancer as well.

Talking about being lost and crushed for words.
Oh boy!

Then my first official poetry book "The Crying Songbird" was finally released worldwide on that Mother's Day. Along with a sold-out book signing at the legendary Walden Bookstore.

Shortly afterwards, I went on to release two more powerful limited-edition books of poetry and storylines. Both entitled "Flying Above All" and "Sunshine with the Rain" vol.1

This eventually led to two more successful book signings at the legendary Barnes & Noble bookstore. Which included an unexpected inclusion and nomination in the very coveted "Who's Who in American Literature" anthology.

Now, when I tell you that the years of 2023 and 2024 have been so beyond epic for me and my team. I literally mean epic!

I am so very honored and elated to have released 6 books that became #1 Best Sellers and International Best Sellers all within a year's time.

However, while I was celebrating these accomplishments, I would also lose three of my dearest loved ones. One of them being my very close cousin Diane Howard aka Lady D, who just so happens to be the Auntie of my deceased cousin Lamar.

Oh Boy, let me tell ya something. I was so beyond heartbroken because she was more than a cousin to me. She was a good friend, a good preschool teacher, a good leader, and a classy woman who loved God dearly. Rest in Peace Lady D. You will be greatly missed, and I really thought that we had more time.

Then we have her beautiful mom, my beloved Aunt Lee RIP, who recently passed away this year, and in the same breath, I was ironically invited to be featured in the "New Jersey Times Top 20 Influential Personalities to Watch for in 2024."

Shortly after that, I got the honor to be featured in the NY Weekly Magazine Top 10 Emerging Celebrities: Sharpening the future of Stardom in 2024. Which also featured Beyoncé, Zendaya and many more. I'm talking about some Sunshine with the Rain.

THE LA TIMES FESTIVAL OF BOOKS: I can still remember this golden moment as if it were yesterday.

Wow, at last I was finally starting to grow as a person, grow as an author, grow as an artist, grow as a father, grow as a writer, grow as a speaker, and grow as an overall leader.

Then suddenly, some big doors began to open up for me and my team, and I'm talking about right in the midst of some of my darkest troubles, darkest trials and darkest tribulations.

I was extremely honored and excited by the opportunity to have one of my first books featured at the LA Times Festival of books, and to have it displayed professionally at one of the most prestigious book events in the world.

So, now my big flight to the west coast was finally booked, and I was beyond ready to fly out to L.A. California, but unfortunately, I would be thrown another curveball in the process.

Before I could even get on the airplane to get settled in. I received an unexpected phone call informing me that my precious grandmother had just passed away. Which was my mom's mother. Rest in Peace Granny

Needless to say, I was very tempted to cancel out the whole event but would instead press forward and turn this deepest pain into my deepest gain growing forward.

However, I was totally devastated inside, and I found myself once again having to take the "ure" off of this word pressure, and then pressing my way forward to go make family history.

I am reminded of an amazing song by the legendary CeCe Winans that says, "It wasn't easy, but it was worth it."

THE MISSOURI BLACK EXPO PRESSURE:
One of my local childhood dreams growing up as a young musician, artist and singer was always to perform and headline at the popular Missouri Black Expo Music Festival.

A very prominent event that featured major urban acts and mainstream talents from all over the country, and when I suddenly got the call to be one of the featured acts.

It was as if another childhood dream of mine had miraculously come to pass.

Yep!

Then it dawned on me that I had visualized this amazing moment countless times in my own subconscious mind repeatedly, and to see it all come to pass and manifesting right before my eyes was nothing less than euphoric and surreal.

Now, I was finally preparing and rehearsing intensely to perform as one of the headliners and opening acts for one of the biggest urban musical festivals in Missouri, and to say that I was excited about it would be an understatement. That's right.

Shortly afterwards, I found out from a few friends that the event promoters had featured one of my records on a radio commercial advertisement and were promoting it in power rotation on one of the biggest radio stations in St. Louis at the time.

Man, I was so beyond pumped and stoked to finally do my thing on this level, and once again another test of high pressure would arise to show its ugly face, and like usual, this typically happened without any warning or any notice.

It was all so sporadic!

I can clearly recall waking up on the morning of the event just to find out that I had no vocals or voice left in me, and boy let me tell you something. It seemed like the perfect moment and opportunity for me to go into a real deep panic mode. You know what I mean?

When I tell you that my voice was totally horse and gone without any sound. I'm telling you the honest to God truth, and to make matters even worse, when we arrived at the Civic Center for the sound check.

I found out that I was no longer just the opening act, but one of the main acts to close out the whole show.

Wow, a big, massive yikes came to my mind very briefly, but fortunately enough I was able to resist the temptation.

So, I left the green room momentarily to get away from everyone. Including my live band and background singers to go pray, and boy, I must have walked around that big civic center at least seven times or more. You know? To shake off the nervousness I was feeling lol.

Can you feel me? Yes sir, I really needed my whole voice back, and I needed it back in a hurry because it was almost show time.

Now, I could have easily panicked and backed out of this high-pressure moment, but I chose to expect the best, leverage the pressure, and then expect a big miracle in return.

After pressing forward continuously, and taking the "ure" off the word pressure. My vocals miraculously returned to me with only five minutes left to go on stage, and let's just say that the big crowd who had shown up to see my live performance. We're not left disappointed at all, and I thank God for that!

PRESSURE IS EVERYWHERE: That's right. Everywhere there is pressure, and it actually takes the pressure in order to grow. I came to the realization that there is no escaping the atmospheres of pressure and pain.

There is just no avoiding it, and I noticed that everything that we do is done under some sort of pressure. We think under pressure, we speak under pressure, we eat under pressure, we learn under pressure, we work under pressure, we breathe under pressure, we love under pressure, and we all grow under pressure as well.

Where there is no pressure, there is no growth. That's right, no pressure, no growth.

Even a pregnant woman needs pressure and pain to birth her baby properly. It is what the doctor means by breathe, breathe, breathe and push, push, push. She must learn how to push, and leverage all her pains, and turn her deepest pains into some of the most beautiful gains possible.

See, a great athlete, a great team, a great artist and a great musician couldn't perform too well without being able to do it all under pressure. Right?

All great entertainers, great leaders, great speakers, and great performers must perform well under pressure, but what does this word pressure really mean?

Pressure is simply the action of a force against another opposing force, and the good news is that all forms of pressure can be leveraged no matter how great or small the pressure is.

GREAT LEADERS HANDLE GREAT PRESSURE: In my humble opinion, the leaders who fold under pressure shouldn't be leading on the front line at all. Because when we fold, others will fold right along with us.
Yep!

John C. Maxwell stated that "Leadership is influence." Which I believe to be very true. Because it is nearly impossible for one to lead without having any impact or influence.

Then I learned that great leadership also comes with great responsibility, and where much is given, much is always required. That's right.

"Leadership is Responsibility."

Now to the best of my knowledge, great leaders are always equipped for handling great pressures. They typically handle the pressures that most people can't.

For example, when my company finds itself under some sort of pressure. It is my absolute duty and responsibility as the leader to take on all of that high pressure for the team, or else how can I properly lead them?

The legendary Brian Tracy said that "To reach your full potential, you must form the habit of putting the pressure on yourself and not waiting for someone else to come along and do it for you."

In other words, great leaders must handle great pressure. Because pressure will always reveal the true fabric of a leader.

CHAPTER 11

My Entrepreneurial Advice in Forbes and GQ

MY FORBES ADVICE: In the year of 2021, after much hard work, and dedication down through the years. Things were finally starting to look up for me and my PME team. As I was so elated to be asked to render some professional advice in the entrepreneur section of Forbes NYC Magazine. The very same issue that featured the legendary Michael Dell on the front cover, and boy I was beyond excited about it.

My personal advice was that it all starts with having a clear vision and mission that can create value for others. Along with having a written game plan to mastermind with your team.

I like to call this my winners circle, and before I attempt to do any big business ventures. I typically start out with prayer and meditation first.

Because it helps me to focus and clear out all of the negative energies.

So, I mentioned that it is very similar to building a new house from the ground up, and that the foundation of that house will always determine its true value, true worth, longevity, and success. Because how we build is how we will live.

That's right!

I went on to say that life and business is all about being able to fully adapt and being able to make the necessary adjustments under very intense pressures. So never give up, and never give in until you win.

"Resilience is Brilliance."

MY GQ ADVICE: In the year of 2021, we were really starting to fly high with a lot of success, and shortly after being featured in the NYC edition of Forbes Magazine with Michael Dell.

I would quickly accept the invitation to be featured in the legendary GQ Magazine. Which also featured the legendary Will Smith on the front cover, and I just couldn't believe and phantom the timing of it all.

Why?

It was merely because this release had dropped around the same time as the Oscar Awards with him and the legendary Chris Rock. Which was a little awkward for me at first considering that I grew up respecting both of their crafts.

However, my entrepreneurial advice at the time was about building a successful dream business that always starts with the foundation of its vision and mission. Quite like the entrepreneurial advice that I gave in the NYC edition of Forbes Magazine.

I told the readers to imagine a successful outcome for their business regardless of the climate shifts surrounding it. Now, some people would call this "The Power of

Visualization." Or envisioning your success before it ever happens.

It is all about launching a business with the right mental attitude and mindset, which will always determine your company's growth and longevity.

You have to simply beat all of the odds that are stacked against you, and I often call this the "Power of beating the odds."

Yep. Meanwhile, I learned that every business had an essence, and that every company had an image that must be clearly defined from the beginning.

This is how we actually define our "why", and this is why I love to pray and meditate first. Because it gives me the strength, wisdom and clarity to clearly understand my why.

Lastly, I told the readers to never be afraid of making the necessary adjustments, and to always be resilient, and to always remain brilliant until the end.

Which are the same exact principles that me and my dream team used to hit #1 in the NY Weekly's Fastest Growing Companies in 2021. Along with being featured in an amazing write up on Broadway World.

CHAPTER 12

Resilience Is Brilliance

KEEP ON GOING, KEEP ON GROWING: Growth is a journey, and not a destination. It is an evolution that never ends, which simply means that we are only growing to grow again.

I can clearly recall those moments when I found myself becoming way too laxed, and way too comfortable with my current results, but then I took notice of how it was starting to stunt my growth. Now don't get me wrong, it is very healthy for us to reflect on our latest accomplishments. However, we should never become too content with where we are.

The legendary Babe Ruth said that "Yesterday's Home Runs Don't Win Today's Game." In other words, I must keep on going and keep on growing hard with the flow.

That's right!

See, most people desire to have big sustainable success, but very few people are willing to grow along the way. Now, let me say that again, "Most people desire to have big sustainable success, but very few people are willing to grow along the way."
"We have to keep on going, and keep on growing until we see our best versions."

True growth is infinite, and it has no final destination but death, and even then, our legacies will live on forever.

Life is like a relay race!

Which is why we must keep on running for as long as we can in order to put the team, the family, and the next generations in a better position to win. The same reason why I can never afford to give up during a very intense race as a leader. Or what hope will that leave for the next runner up?

So, I finally came to the conclusion that if I gave up, someone else would eventually give up too.

Now, have you ever seen a runner racing for the Olympic gold medal run off of the track because of their fatigue? Nope, and you probably never will. Some of the most powerful people in the universe are those who possess great resilience and perseverance. The resilient ones who never give up and quit whereas most people do, and I decided many years ago that I would never give up on myself nor give up on my biggest dreams. Nope!

After all, the race is not given to the swift nor to the strong, but to the one who endures until the end. Now you may be asking, what in the world does this word resilience mean?

Well, I'm so glad that you asked me!

Resilience is the capacity to withstand or recover quickly from difficult situations, and it means having the mental toughness and tenacity during the toughest moments of your life, and to always prosper in any environment.

A wise man once said, "Greatness takes time, it takes time to build your brand, it takes time to build your life, it takes time to build your career. So be resilient, stick it out, winter, spring, summer, and fall. You must be prepared to get a thousand no's just to get one yes."

Because our setbacks are merely comebacks in disguise.

KEEP THE BIG DREAM ALIVE: Some big dreams will live, and some big dreams will surely die, but it is our job to keep them alive.

It was a blessing to finally become aware of all the big dream killers surrounding me, and a lot of the time they were hanging out right in my own backyard.
Those individuals who were only small thinkers, and small dreamers by nature. Who only wanted me to settle for less, and to not fly beyond their expectations of me. So, I did it anyway. That's right! Dream big anyway, live big anyway, and do it big unapologetically.

I liken my dreams to that of a human life. Meaning that it has a pulse, a heartbeat, a brain, and a voice that speaks directly to the soul. Very similar to a body that functions by way of its muscles, blood cells, veins, and oxygen supply. Which reminds of a difficult time when my dreams almost died on life support.

Woe!

Imagine for a brief moment, your newborn child dying on life support due to a lack of nutrition, and many times this is how we will nurture our own dreams.

Inadvertently, we starve them out without ever realizing that these dreams will have to be nurtured, and we do this by feeding them with our goals.

That's right!

The consistent goals that we set will essentially become our roadmap to success, but unfortunately, we allow them to be conceived into our minds, conceived into our hearts, and yet we fail to realize that there is a due date for all those big dreams to be born. In other words, we miscarriage our dreams.

So, by any means necessary, keep the big dream alive. Even if it doesn't happen in your lifetime. Because a big dream of value will always outlive the dreamer. Just ask MLK. RIP

THE LAW OF RESILIENCE: Is simply the law of recovery, and it is the master key to all success. So, when I feel like quitting, I just don't. That is the law! The Legendary Hank Aaron said that,

"My motto was always to keep on swinging whether I was in a slump or feeling badly or having trouble off the field, the only thing to do was keep swinging." So, we have to keep on swinging until the wheels fall off, and even then, we should always be willing to grow a little bit further the next time.

Because growth is a journey and an evolution that never ends.
Now, let me say that once again. I said, "Growth is a journey and an evolution that never ends."

Do you recall me saying that earlier?

Which is why I tend to do the very opposite of quitting, and in return I receive more and more momentum. Sure, we all feel like quitting sometimes and throwing in the towel. It is simply us being human, or one just being a human being.

So, what do you do when you feel like giving up and throwing in the towel? Well, the answer is quite simple.

You don't!

You just keep on growing with the flow and find every reason under the sun to never give up. The great MLK said, "Giving up is easy and continuing is hard, choose your hard and make a firm decision. If you can't fly then run, if you can't run then walk, if you can't walk then crawl, but whatever you do, you must keep moving forward. That's right!

I am now reminded of an amazing story about Pharaoh and his army who came up against the children of Israel, and when things looked hopeless.

They all started to panic right along with their leader Moses for a moment.

However, when Moses would make the proper mind shift. He then told the children of Israel to be still, to stop panicking, and then to go forward and visualize their deliverance, and only then could they witness the red sea departing miraculously to cross over on dry ground.

WHEN YOUR CLOSEST PEOPLE CHANGE: Some people will always evolve and change on you without warning. So please don't be alarmed.

The one thing that I noticed on my quest for having major success is that success will organically expose the true characters of the closest people around you. You will gradually start to notice the ones who were genuinely for you. Right along with noticing the ones who were genuinely not.

However, the truth is that the spotlight falls upon everyone and everything simultaneously, and the things that get exposed are totally inexplicable. So, buckle up baby!
See, once you start flying to higher heights, and achieving new levels.

Everyone's true colors will automatically unveil, and this includes family too.

I can clearly recall meeting a very famous leader in Los Angeles, California a few years back in a gym who had appeared on national TV. I had just landed to attend the LA Times Festival of Books to have my first book featured, and the dope thing about it was that she read my book and gave it a great review.

Wow!

She was very encouraging, and very knowledgeable about the business of arts and entertainment too. So, I just had to pick her brain a little with some burning questions.

Then I asked, "Why does it seem as if some of your closest people, or even your family members will start changing once you start making it?"

And she replied "Well, welcome to the entry level of fame and celebrity Willie J. It just comes with the turf little brother, and trust me I can totally relate to how you're feeling right now."
For the mere fact that the same thing happened to me while I was being featured on the Bill Cosby show, and on the front covers of some famous magazines. So much so that some of my closest family members failed to show up at my big wedding.

Wow! Talking about being totally bombed out!

I was completely blown away by this sad news, but at the same time it encouraged me to know that I wasn't alone. You know?

In a nutshell she was letting me know to just keep on growing forward, and to never stop winning no matter what.

THE VIRTUE OF PATIENCE: I soon discovered that people, places, things, and seasons are all temporary, and are always subject to change. Because nothing ever stays the same. So why even worry about it right?

Over time, I had to learn how to go along with God's timing instead of going backwards by timing God. Yep!

The cure for all anxiety is the ability to possess more patience while growing forward, and to have the capacity to wait and be still when it is necessary.
For it is written that we should never be anxious for nothing. Because when we are anxious about things. It will only lead to

more frustrations, fear, worry, and uncertainty.

That's right! It can only lead to anxiety.

However, I know that this is easier said than done, but the more patient we are, the less anxious we are, and the less anxious we are, the more peaceful we are.

We must come to a firm resolution that anything in this life is worth having will always take time. You know the famous saying, "Rome wasn't built overnight" but what does this word patience really mean?

I learned that patience is the capacity to accept or tolerate delay, trouble, or suffering without getting angry or upset. It is the frequency of our faith, and the endurance of our belief system.
The legendary Joyce Meyers said that "Patience is a fruit of the spirit that grows only under trial."

Which is very true, considering that most of my patience came through many hardships. Yelp!

I can totally appreciate the fact that my success didn't happen overnight. Because the brutal truth is that I wouldn't have been able to handle it.

See, sometimes we can desire the right things at the wrong time or desire the best things at the worst time, and we must fully comprehend that God's timing is everything. Yep!

The one thing that I have learned about living in this microwave society is that people don't like to wait for things for too long. They always want it now, and they always want it quick and easy. Which is simply a microwave mindset.

However, if you take notice that a baby or a child will not skip ages during their growth cycle. Neither will you see a one-year-old baby growing right into being a five-year-old suddenly. They have to grow day by day, month by month, and year by year. True growth will always take time.

MAMA MADE LA WEIGHT LOSS HISTORY: It was on a very sunny day in Fairview Heights, Illinois, and I had just arrived at my mom's house where I was living at the time, and as I walked through the door. She greeted me with some of the most amazing news ever.

She was so beyond elated and excited to tell me that she had finally hit the jackpot, and that she had made LA Weight Loss history.

Now mind you, my mom was very deep into health and fitness at the time, but this massive achievement was a brand-new milestone for her to say the least.

They were about to fly her down to Los Angeles, California to feature her on one of their biggest billboards, and to also feature her in a national commercial. Wow!

I couldn't have been more excited for my mom. Because all her hard work and dedication had finally paid off big time, and I literally watched my beautiful Mama turn her resilience right into historic brilliance. But unfortunately, she died of breast cancer before she could ever live this dream out, but never forgotten. Rest in Heaven Mama!

KNOW THE VISION, GROW THE VISION: I discovered that you must know the vision, in order to grow the vision, and in order to grow the vision you have to know the vision.

We can't grow what we don't know, and it is written that, "Without a vision the people will perish."

Now, imagine me trying to drive forward on the road in a moving vehicle or a motorcycle blindfolded in some oncoming traffic. What do you think the outcome would be?

Well, I believe that it would be something very horrific, or even worse tragic. Which brings me to my main point here. The very reason why most people's dreams suddenly die and collapse. Simply because their dreams have no vision. Yep!

So, I soon discovered that there is something very powerful about writing out our biggest dreams on paper, and we often call this,

"Thinking in Ink."

That's right, when we write out our biggest goals, game plans, and strategies. We are literally thinking in ink at that point.

Then I eventually learned how to write out the vision to make it plain enough for me and the whole team to grow it forward. In other words, I had to know the vision to grow the vision.

Now let me say that again,

"I had to know the vision in order to grow the vision" and I have to know it like the back of my hand when no one else does. Which was the same exact concept that we used to write out the vision and mission statement for Pure Mission Entertainment.

Then as a leader of influence, I would have to delete the need of always being understood by others, and then erase the need for outside validation and acceptance. Because everyone will never understand the vision.

The legendary Brianna Weist said that "Your new life is going to cost you being loved and understood." In other words, get over worrying about what others think of you, and always continue to be the champion that God created you to be. Never lose sight of that.

BUILDING A WINNING FOUNDATION: Without a solid foundation there is nothing to build upon. So, anytime that we think of the word growth, we should automatically think of the word foundation.

Because in order to have a winning company one must first have a winning foundation along with having a winning team.

After all it takes teamwork to make the dreams work, right? Yes!

A strong winning team is one of the most essential elements for having major success and massive achievement. So, no team, no dream, and when we are building up our team, we are literally building up our foundation simultaneously.

Now with that being said: I am now reminded of a great parable about the two-house builders who built their houses upon two different types of foundations. One house was built upon a winning foundation and the other house was built upon a losing one.

The first builder had decided to build his house upon a weak foundation with sinking sand because of his lack of application. Then when the winds and the storms came about to blow up against this house. It soon came tumbling down with a hard fall without the possibility of recovery.

However, the other house builder heard these same sets of instructions and decided to build his house upon a solid rock through consistent application, and when those same winds and storms came about to blow up against his house. It withstood the test of time simply because of its solid foundation.

Now speaking of the word foundation, what does it really mean in commentary?

A foundation is the basis or the groundwork of anything that functions. It is the fact, principle or idea that provides support for a thing.

See, the only way to win big, and keep on winning in any field of business is to keep on building it upon a winning foundation, and remember as I mentioned before,

"How we build is how we live."

NEVER FORGET THE 3 LAWS OF WINNING: There will always be certain laws and precepts for big winning, and if we break these laws we will simply lose out in the end.

Ok, now let's go back to the three laws of winning for a minute. All the greatest achievers in life possess these same three laws.

Which is simply taking actions, gaining traction, and then gaining attraction over time, and if you notice that in all the three movements the word action is spelled out three times. Yep!

Now if you take the "tr" off of the word traction, and then take the "attr" off of the word attraction. You are still left with the word action which is mentioned three times. So let us always remember that it takes consistent actions to gain traction, and it takes consistent traction in order to gain the necessary attractions growing forward.

LIFE IS ALL ABOUT BEGINNING AGAIN: For some things to begin, some things must surely end. There can be no beginnings without endings, and there can be no endings without beginnings.

In this life we will always face endings and beginnings, and it's never too late for one to start over, reset, and win big beyond their wildest dreams.

It ain't over until it's over.

I am a living testament of this truth, and my most painful endings became some of my most beautiful beginnings over time.

DEVELOPING THE COURAGE TO WIN: Eventually, I began to notice that courage was one of my superpowers, and it eventually became one of my greatest assets for having success too. That's right, courage is one of my greatest assets, and it is the biggest muscle behind all my biggest dreams.

The legendary Maya Angelou said that "Courage is the most important of all the virtues, because without courage you cannot practice any other virtue consistently. So, you build your courage muscle by being courageous in small things."

Now, this is how we "Never Stop Winning." To be continued...

A Call to Action:

WHERE DO I GROW NEXT? Actions breed actions and growth breeds growth. I wonder, have you ever felt like giving up on your own personal growth journey due to a lack of results? Or maybe you are ready to leave that negative past behind you once and for all to finally become the best version of yourself?

Now, if that's you, I would like to sincerely invite you to a life changing workshop event that is entitled, "Win Your Way". Which is really God's way at the end of the day!

The "Win Your Way" workshop is where we will take you through an amazing process of kingdom empowerment and self-discovery based on the winning principles inside of this book. This is hosted by me, and facilitated by the Legendary Richard Mover who is also a Maxwell Leadership coach, and a PME team advisor.

So, we look forward to seeing you there on the inside, and for more information please visit us at the websites below.

https://winyourwayworkshops.com
https://puremissionent.com
https://williejpmebookings.com/

You can also look out for the global launching of my new "Never Stop Winning" Radio Show, courtesy of the "Walking Out Purpose Radio Network". airing in all 195 Countries worldwide. I would like to give a huge shout out to the legendary CEO Kayla Padgett for making all this possible, and to my amazing client, and friend Arthur Flash Johnson for bringing us together!

Much love to each and every one of you from around the globe who purchased this book. I wish you nothing but the best in abundance throughout the course of your spiritual and personal growth journey. Peace, Love, and Blessings to you always.

Dedications & Thank You's:

I would like to first thank my personal Lord and Savior Jesus Christ for always being Paramount in my life, and for equipping me with the divine strength and wherewithall to finish up this book. For I am nothing without you, but I am everything with you, and I mean this in the most intimate way!

To my amazing President Aaron Emig and the whole PME Dream Team for always believing in me, and for tirelessly investing in the vision that God gave me. Then to my MD crew Theo, Louis, and 88. The value that you add to me is second to none, and I am always beyond grateful for you all.

To my good friends Steve Kidd, and Richard Mover for your undying support of my vision and mission, and to all my co-authoring buddies world wide. It was so amazing hitting multiple #1 International Bestsellers with you, and empowering so many lives from around the globe. You know who you are. A big special thanks to the #1 International Best-Selling "Winning

With Love" Dream Team. Kinga Vajda, Nancy Debra Barrow, Brian Schulman, Jacuqeline Diaz, LS Kirkpatrick, Judy Lynn, Steve Kidd, and Dr. Deepak Bhootra. Thank you for joining me.

To my amazing editors and marketing team. You are all so beyond amazing and dope. I can't thank you enough for capturing all my writings, and for helping me to bring them more to life. Thank you so much for always adding value to me. We are changing the world together.

Now, to all my personal assistants, managers, global media, TV networks, DJs, engineers, radio stations, sponsors, magazines and social media followers worldwide. I really appreciate your unfailing love and support. To my legendary friend Dr. Monica R. Butler courtesy of the Gospel Music Hall of Fame. I really appreciate the nomination sis, and our best is yet to come.

To the legendary Dr. Forbes Riley, and to my good buddy Cardinal Cowboy for featuring me multiple times on his amazing TV show courtesy of ABC30. Then to the Level Up Academy, and the amazing Voice Your Vibe Tribe. I always appreciate your love and support.

Ok, last but not least to my anointed father Pastor Willie B. Jones Jr. Love you always mighty man of God, and don't you ever stop winning.

Finally, to my beautiful Mom Barbara Ann Jones, and to the beautiful Godmothers of PME. Camille F. Emig-Hill and Helen P. Harden. Thank you so much for all of your love and support down through the years. This one's for you. Love Always. R.I.P.

This book is sincerely dedicated to all of the victims who have been greatly affected by Breast Cancer.

Photos taken by: Raynard Nicholson

Made in the USA
Monee, IL
04 October 2025